MW01118758

To Eric R.

With best regards ..

this book is of interest to yo...

and your compatriots.

Respectfully,

Robert V. Stuart

804-462-7894

ALL IN THE
RECORD

ONE COUPLE'S FIGHT TO
EXPOSE DECEIT IN
LANCASTER COUNTY,
VIRGINIA

ROBERT V. SMART

This book is a work of non-fiction. Unless otherwise noted, the author and the publisher make no explicit guarantees as to the accuracy of the information contained in this book and in some cases, names of people and places have been altered to protect their privacy.

Scripture taken from the King James Version of the Bible

LifeRich Publishing is a registered trademark of The Reader's Digest Association, Inc.

LifeRich Publishing books may be ordered through booksellers or by contacting:

LifeRich Publishing
1663 Liberty Drive
Bloomington, IN 47403
www.liferichpublishing.com
1 (888) 238-8637

Because of the dynamic nature of the Internet, any web addresses or links contained in this book may have changed since publication and may no longer be valid. The views expressed in this work are solely those of the author and do not necessarily reflect the views of the publisher, and the publisher hereby disclaims any responsibility for them.

Any people depicted in stock imagery provided by Getty Images are models, and such images are being used for illustrative purposes only. Certain stock imagery © Getty Images.

ISBN: 978-1-4897-2266-9 (sc)
ISBN: 978-1-4897-2267-6 (hc)
ISBN: 978-1-4897-2271-3 (e)

Library of Congress Control Number: 2019941615

Print information available on the last page.

LifeRich Publishing rev. date: 05/02/2019

This is a documented study describing events that should not have happened. These events might not have happened with better awareness. If better awareness comes through this book, then the book has achieved its purpose.

This book is founded on two sets of public records. The first set is land records held in the Records Room at Lancaster Courthouse, Virginia. The second set is court records of proceedings in Lancaster Circuit Court that are now kept in the Library of Virginia. The land records span a period of almost one and a half centuries. The court records come from two different proceedings. The first proceeding is a hearing held on April 9, 1912 that resulted in a consent decree to subdivide a farm. The second proceeding is a jury trial held on September 11, 2014 that undoes the work of the earlier court. Two months after the 2014 trial it is proven through old land records that pivotal testimony given to the jury is false. The false testimony derives from a land survey done in 1975 which is inconsistent with several deeds recorded long before the survey was done.

The author's life became inextricably enmeshed in events leading to the 2014 trial. From this evolves a dramatic narrative that is woven into the factual development.

This book may be of great interest to judges, legislators, attorneys, real estate agents and land surveyors. But anyone who owns land should read this book for useful insights.

CONTENTS

INTRODUCTION

The quiet of our estates, in a great measure, depends upon the faithfulness, understanding, and care of our surveyors.

Virginia Statutes, 1705

This is a true story founded on deeds and surveys archived in the Records Room at Lancaster Courthouse in Lancaster, Virginia. In addition to the recorded deeds and surveys, there are two very important documents arising from a proceeding heard in Lancaster Circuit Court on April 9, 1912. The court documents are now kept at the Library of Virginia in Richmond. A number of exhibits are referenced in the text and shown at the end of this book. The exhibits support the narrative by offering more complete understanding, but careful study of the exhibits is not necessary to follow the story.

The geographic setting for this book is St. Mary's White Chapel District of Lancaster County, on the Northern Neck of Virginia. The Northern Neck is a narrow peninsula lying between the lengthy tidal estuaries of the Potomac and the Rappahannock Rivers. The Northern Neck is an inland marine environment, located on the western shore of Chesapeake Bay, where land and water merge to form a kayaker's paradise.

My name is Robert Smart. My involvement in this story began in 1971, when I first bought land on the Northern Neck. I was still young and single when in 1973 I bought additional land adjoining my first land purchase. In 1975 I made the wisest decision of my life.

I married Miss Jena Ann Beckman. From the outset of our marriage Jena and I dreamed of living on our Virginia land. But my career as a commissioned officer of the United States made us wait many years to realize our dream. In 1996 I retired after thirty years of commissioned service, which was split between the United States Navy and the Commissioned Officer Corps of the National Oceanic and Atmospheric Administration (NOAA). Jena and I began our move to the Northern Neck immediately after I retired.

Seventeen years after I retired a survey was done of land adjoining the tract I had bought in 1973. In the course of his work the surveyor, Mr. Michael A. Wind, set a stake at the southeast corner of the land he was surveying. This stake also marked the southwest corner of Jena's and my land. In fact, the stake marked the common point for three properties that had been created by a consent decree of Lancaster Circuit Court on April 9, 1912. The geographic position of Mr. Wind's stake is shown as the center of the circle drawn on the copy of Section 20 of the Lancaster County Tax Map presented at the end of this introduction. The hachured areas labeled "CBTB" and "Heritage Point" on the tax map indicate two large residential waterfront communities. The subject area for this book is the land that lies between those two residential communities.

I first observed Mr. Wind's corner stake on the evening of Thursday, March 28, 2013, as I was departing my property en route to choir practice at church. Later that night I wrote on my calendar: "*DRIVEWAY STAKE*?" I made this entry because I was immediately aware upon seeing the stake of an inconsistency between the location of Mr. Wind's stake and the southwest corner of Jena's and my land as shown on three previous certified land surveys done by the land surveying company Tomlin and Keyser, Inc. Because of the previous surveys Jena and I were initially skeptical about the placement of Mr. Wind's stake. But the inconsistency spurred me to begin research. My research has now extended into six years and many events have occurred since I first saw that stake. While it has been fascinating for

Jena and me to acquire a better understanding of the history of this area through our research, it has been challenging to write this book tying together information contained in records filed at various times during three different centuries. Jena and I hope the results of our research will prove interesting to and will provide useful information for the reader.

This story involves some technicalities of land surveying. I have tried to reduce such technicality in the narrative, but some of that is unavoidable. Here is information useful to understanding this story. First, there is the matter of angular measurements. There are 60 seconds (″) of arc in one minute (′) of arc; there are 60 minutes (′) of arc in 1 degree (°) of arc; and there are 360 degrees (°) of arc in a closed circle. A right angle is one-quarter of a circle, or ninety degrees (90°) of arc. Land surveyors generally use the degree, minute, and second (DMS) format rather than decimal portions of a degree in their work. Thus, a land surveyor would describe a right angle as 90°00′00″, rather than as 90.0000°. Angles can be added and subtracted in the DMS format by remembering the "sixty" basis for minutes and seconds of arc, just as for minutes and seconds of time. Surveyors label bearings by ninety degree quadrants, as northeast (NE), southeast (SE), southwest (SW), or northwest (NW). For example, a bearing taken 45 degrees east of north would be in the northeast quadrant and would be written as N 45°00′00″ E.

Older surveys, because instruments then were not as fine as today's instruments, give bearings as degrees and fractions of a degree rather than as degrees, minutes, and seconds. For example, the bearing N 45°30′ 00″ E would appear in an old survey as N 45 ½ E.

The second technical concept is that of closure. The concept of a boundary survey of a tract of land is well defined by regulation. When a boundary survey is conducted, the surveyor must begin the survey at some point on the boundary of the tract being surveyed and then traverse the entire perimeter of the tract being surveyed to close the survey by returning to the same point. The need for closure is intuitive because a parcel of land is not defined until its boundaries are closed. If closure is not achieved, it is not possible to determine the area (acreage) of a tract. Virginia Code is very specific about the technical requirements for closure of a boundary survey. Those requirements are given in Virginia Code 18VAC10-20-370. The same code describes the requirements for monumentation of a boundary survey. The code requires that a lasting object must be sited at every bend in the line of a boundary survey. If closure is not accomplished within the tolerances required, then a proper boundary survey has not been conducted and no acreage should be certified.

I graduated from the United States Naval Academy (USNA) in June 1966. My graduation occurred soon after the beginning of United States military involvement in Vietnam. After two tours of duty in the Vietnam Theater, I transferred my commission to the United States Coast and Geodetic Survey (USC&GS). Within a few years the Commissioned Officer Corps of the USC&GS became the Commissioned Officer Corps of the newly created National Oceanic and Atmospheric Administration (NOAA). NOAA Corps officers are subject to national defense service through a memorandum of understanding between the Department of Defense and the Department of Commerce. During the course of my career with NOAA I was assigned on occasion to lead hydrographic surveys. Prior to operation of the global positioning system it was necessary to establish ground control by geodetic land survey in order to tie offshore soundings to land. I received training to accomplish such geodetic control surveys.

Jena and I have two children. Our son, Jason, is a registered professional engineer working with the American Wood Council in Leesburg, Virginia. He and his wife, Suzanne, both have engineering degrees from Virginia Tech. Our daughter, Tammy, is a registered dietitian nutritionist who works in Richmond, Virginia.

Section 20-Lancaster county tax map

CHAPTER 1
Story of a Civil War Veteran

Louis Oscar Cox was born on February 2, 1847. He was only 18 years old when he returned home, a survivor of the Civil War. Louis had served honorably in Company H, Fortieth Regiment, Virginia Infantry. After his return home, young Louis married Miss Elnora Biscoe, and the couple settled on land which Elnora inherited from her mother, Mrs. Nancy Biscoe. In 1882 Louis and Elnora bought additional land from their neighbors, Mr. Warner W. and Mrs. Mary A. Beane. They paid $341.84 for the adjoining land on May 15, 1882. To finance their purchase they borrowed from the Glebe Fund of Lancaster. Louis and Elnora's farm was located on a small rise called Sage Hill, located in St. Mary's White Chapel District, which is in the western part of Lancaster County, Virginia. Access to their farm was by a wagon road leading up Sage Hill from River Road, just south of a little village called Woodbine. The name Woodbine was later changed to Molusk because there were too many post offices in the United States named Woodbine. Still later the spelling of Molusk was changed to the more proper form of Mollusk. That name derives from the plentiful oysters of phylum *mollusca* that are especially tasty in the shallow, lower salinity tidal waters of Lancaster County.

Louis and Elnora worked hard to make a success of their farm and to raise their three daughters, whom they named Mary (nicknamed Mamie), Rosa, and Fannie.

But life was difficult for the Cox family because economic vitality returned slowly to the South after the Civil War. The development of Virginia's public roads, beginning early in the 1900s, spurred economic growth. During that time the state acquired a thirty foot wide right-of-way along the old wagon road leading up Sage Hill. This road was designated Virginia State Highway 662 (VSH 662). In 1988, the right-of-way for VSH 662 was widened from thirty feet to forty feet. Later, the road was paved and it was named Sage Hill Road. But all of this occurred long after Louis and Elnora Cox had passed away.

Louis and Elnora kept a loving home. While they were not wealthy, the family was healthy and happy. Louis worked hard to make a success of the Cox farm, but it never did well financially. Louis was just able to provide basic necessities for his family. Most importantly, he failed to meet the financial obligations he had incurred in buying the Beane's land. Three decades after taking out the loan, Louis had not paid any of the $341.84 principal, and over three decades the interest in arrears had grown to $89.00 dollars. The sum of $430.84 may not seem like much in terms of today's devalued dollars, but that was a lot of money for a poor farmer in the early 1900s. The reality was that Louis Oscar Cox had a serious financial problem.

Then disaster struck. Louis and Elnora's daughter, Mamie, passed away on October 8, 1907, at just 28 years of age. Mamie left behind her husband, Mr. E. F. Haynie, and four young children. The youngest child, Nellie, was newborn. A few years later Elnora passed away without leaving a will. Soon the Trustees of the Glebe Fund were asking Louis about the 1882 loan. By then, Louis was sixty-four years old, widowed, living alone, and deeply in debt. The Civil War veteran had seen danger and hard work throughout his life, but he had little material wealth to show for it. His legacy to Lancaster County would be the family he left behind.

Fortunately, two of Louis's daughters, Rosa and Fannie, lived nearby with their families. Louis realized he couldn't keep up with heavy farm work too much longer, and he also knew that even if he could keep up with the work, it probably would not pay enough to satisfy his debt. Louis wanted to get out of debt and to help his son-in-law, Mr. Haynie, to care for his four children: Louis, Elnora, McClinnock, and Nellie. Louis also wanted to give something to Rosa and her husband, Mr. Ned Thomas; and to Fannie and her husband, Mr. William Streets. After some thought, Louis came up with a plan. He called a family meeting to present it. He proposed to divide his eighty-six acre farm. He would retain a portion of the land, and the remainder would be divided into thirds for Mamie's family, Rosa's family, and Fannie's family. Mr. Haynie and Fannie agreed to sell their thirds and to give Louis a portion of the proceeds. Rosa and Ned Thomas chose to pay the same portion to Louis in order to retain Rosa's one-third share. In this way, every member of the Cox family benefited and Mr. Cox could pay his debt and remain in his home. The family agreed with the plan.

Mr. Raymond E. Dobyns, the twenty-five year old son of a neighboring family, heard of the plan and expressed a desire to purchase Mr. Haynie's and Mrs. Fannie Streets's one-third shares. A young attorney named Thomas J. Downing was asked to draft an agreement for the Cox Family and for Mr. Dobyns. Because the interests of minor children were involved, the agreement had to be approved by Lancaster Circuit Court.

On April 9, 1912, Mr. T. J. Downing, Mr. L. O. Cox, Mr. R. E. Dobyns, Mrs. R. E. Thomas, Mr. E. F. Haynie, Mrs. F. D. Streets, and Mr. P. M. Gresham, acting as the guardian ad litem for the children, met in Lancaster Circuit Court to ask for approval of the agreement. After hearing the request, the court asked another attorney, Mr. Robert O.

Norris Jr., to research the benefits of the agreement for all interested parties and to report back that day if possible. Mr. R. O. Norris Jr. did a quick review and reported back the same day that the agreement was beneficial to all parties. The court then issued a decree approving the agreement and named Mr. T. J. Downing as special commissioner to draft the deeds necessary to execute the agreement. Mr. Downing was ordered to report his proceedings to the next term of the court.

Exhibit 1-1 shows the Cox Farm as it existed in October 1911. The land within the trapezoid is the Cox farm, and it is described in the agreement as "eighty-six acres that have been used as one farm." The agreement, typed from a handwritten document archived at the Library of Virginia, is given as exhibit 1-2. The consent decree to the agreement, also typed from a handwritten document archived at the Library of Virginia, is given as exhibit 1-3.

After the breakup of his farm, Mr. Louis Oscar Cox went on to live a second phase of life. In his sixties, Louis married a beautiful young lady. Their marriage was short, however, for on June 14, 1917 Mr. Cox died of pneumonia at the age of seventy. Mr. Cox is buried in Bethel United Methodist Church Cemetery on St. Mary's White Chapel Road (VSH 201) near Lively, Virginia.

I was extremely fortunate in 1973 to befriend one of Mr. Louis Oscar Cox's grandchildren – a woman named Margaret Thomas Mallory. Margaret was the daughter of Ned and Rosa Thomas. In her last year of life, Margaret's memory was keen. She loved to relate stories about the community where she grew up in the early 1900s. Within a short time of meeting her, I came to admire Margaret. I was an avid listener to the stories she told of the community where she grew up.

Within two weeks of Louis's death, soldiers and marines from both the north and the south began to arrive in France. Under the command of Major General John J. "Black Jack" Pershing those men fought bravely "over there" to end the trauma of World War I. After

World War I and World War II had ended, and after all Civil War veterans had passed away, Congress enacted US Public Law 85-425, Section 410 on May 28, 1958. That law states:

"CONFEDERATE FORCES VETERANS"

"Sec. 410. The Administrator shall pay to each person who served in the military or naval forces of the Confederate States of America during the Civil War a monthly pension in the same amounts and subject to the same conditions as would have been applicable to such person under the laws in effect on December 31, 1957, if his service in such forces had been service in the military or naval forces of the United States."

This law benefited a few elderly widows of Confederate veterans. Unfortunately the law came forty-one years too late to benefit Louis Oscar Cox. But it is interesting to imagine how different this story might have been if Mr. Cox had received benefits during his lifetime. He might have been able to better provide for his family and to hold his farm together.

Every Memorial Day the men of Bethel United Methodist Church place small US flags on the graves of all veterans buried in Bethel Cemetery near lively, Virginia. The grave of Confederate veteran Louis Oscar Cox is so honored. From what Margaret told me about her grandfather, I believe Mr. Cox would be pleased with what the United States of America has become in the one hundred and two years since his death.

CHAPTER 2

The Downing Deeds

Less than a week after Lancaster Circuit Court approved the Cox farm subdivision, the British steamship *Titanic* sank on its maiden voyage. The ship had been advertised as unsinkable, so the public was shocked that 1,595 people died when the ship foundered within hours of striking an iceberg. The tragedy was still the talk of the community when Mr. Thomas J. Downing sat down on April 30, 1912 to draft the deeds subdividing the Cox Farm. The Lancaster Circuit Court had appointed Mr. Downing as special commissioner to draft those deeds, and it had instructed him "to report his proceedings under the decree to the next term of this Court." By the thirtieth of April time was running short, so Mr. Downing concentrated his efforts to write three deeds of conveyance and one deed of trust on that day. By his first deed, Mr. Downing conveyed "twenty and three quarters of an acre by actual survey" of the eighty-six acres he was subdividing. This was the curtesy retention of Mr. Louis O. Cox. Those twenty and three quarter acres had been surveyed the previous year on July 3, 1911 by Mr. Herbert P. Hall, the county surveyor. Mr. Hall's survey had been cited by the court in its decree approving the subdivision, and Mr. Downing included the survey as part of the deed he wrote to Mr. Cox (exhibit 2-2, page 2). A few days later, Mr. Downing personally recorded that deed in the Lancaster County land records.

By his second deed, Mr. Downing conveyed "twenty-three and three quarter acres" to Mrs. Rosa E. Thomas. There is some question about the statement of acreage conveyed. It is likely that Mr. Downing intended to convey only twenty-one and three quarter acres. But Mr. Downing twice states the acreage as twenty-three and three quarter acres. In writing the deed to Mrs. Thomas, Mr. Downing refers to the Hall survey as he describes the boundary between the land he conveys to Mrs. Rosa E. Thomas and the land he conveys in the next deed he writes to Mr. Raymond E. Dobyns. Mr. Downing's description is very clear, but this boundary will come into question one hundred and one years later.

In his third deed, Mr. Downing does not state the acreage conveyed to Mr. Raymond E. Dobyns. But in the deed of trust that Mr. Downing drafts immediately after writing the deed of conveyance, he describes the acreage of the tract that Mr. Dobyns is buying as "forty-three acres, be the same more or less". This creates a situation that is inconsistent with the subdivision agreement. Here is why. From the deeds that Mr. T. J. Downing wrote, the total acreage conveyed is eighty-seven and one half acres, as follows: first, twenty and three quarter acres to Mr. Cox; second, twenty-three and three quarter acres to Mrs. Thomas; and finally, the forty-three acres described in the deed of trust to Mr. Dobyns. Looking more carefully at what the agreement says about division of the Cox farm, it is clear that Mr. L. O. Cox is first to receive the twenty and three quarter acres (20 ¾ acres) surveyed by Mr. H. P. Hall. Then the remainder of the eighty-six acre (86 acre) farm, which is sixty-five and one quarter acres (65 ¼ acres), is to be divided so that Mrs. Rosa Thomas receives one-third of the remainder, or twenty-one and three quarter acres (21 ¾ acres), and Mr. Raymond Dobyns receives two-thirds of the remainder, or forty-three and one half acres (43 ½ acres). In this manner the three parcels created by the subdivision of the eighty-six acre farm would total eighty-six acres. For the analysis rendered in this book, it will be assumed that the conveyances intended by Mr. T. J. Downing are as stipulated in the agreement.

Exhibit 2-1 shows how Mr. T. J. Downing divided the Cox farm on April 30, 1912. Exhibit 2-2 is a photocopy of the deed Mr. Downing wrote to Mr. L. O. Cox. Please note that Mr. Downing included a drawing of the survey done by Mr. Herbert P. Hall as part of the first deed he wrote. Mr. Downing probably did this because the court decree specified that the conveyance to Mr. Cox was to be "in accordance with the survey recently made, plat of which said survey has been shown to the Court." Also, it is very important that Mr. Downing included and recorded the Hall survey as part of his special commissioner work because Mr. Hall's survey is the key to subdivision of the Cox farm. Mr. Hall's survey is integral to subdivision of the Cox farm because all internal boundaries among the three conveyances arising from the subdivision depend on Mr. Hall's survey.

Exhibit 2-3 is a photocopy of the second deed Mr. Downing wrote on April 30, 1912. This deed is to Mrs. Rosa Thomas, and in this deed Mr. Downing gives a very clear description of the boundary between the land he is conveying to Mrs. Thomas and the land he will convey in the next deed he writes to Mr. Raymond Dobyns. Here is that description:

> *"The westward boundary is yet to be established by a survey of the land hereby conveyed which said westward boundary is to run at right angles to the line of the land of the said L. O. Cox as same has heretofore been surveyed and for that purpose reference is hereby made to the plat of said Coxes land made by H. P. Hall dated July 3, 1911 and of record with the deed of said L. O. Cox. To have and to hold the said twenty-three and three quarters acres of land with their appurtenances to her the said Rosa E. Thomas and her heirs and assigns forever."*

Mr. Downing further describes the bounds of the conveyance to Mrs. Rosa Thomas as follows:

"On the north by the lands of Moton Tomlin and lands of Mrs. C. C. Chilton, on the east by Senior Creek and the lands of C. M. Beane, and on the south by the lands this day conveyed to L. O. Cox, and on the west by the land this day conveyed to R. E. Dobyns by T. J. Downing, Special Commissioner."

Exhibit 2-4 is a photocopy of the deed of conveyance Mr. Downing wrote to Mr. Raymond E. Dobyns. (Exhibit 2-4 also includes the deed of trust Mr. Dobyns was required to provide.) By the deed of conveyance Mr. Raymond Dobyns receives title to the share of the Cox farm that Mr. E. F. Haynie and his children (Mamie's one-third share) were selling, and to the share of the Cox farm that Mr. and Mrs. William Streets (Fannie's one-third share) were selling. In the deed of conveyance to Mr. Raymond Dobyns, Mr. Downing wrote:

"The eastern boundary is to be established between said R. E. Dobyns and Rosa E. Thomas as same is provided for in deed this day made by said T. J. Downing to said Rosa E. Thomas, to which said deed reference is hereby made."

Thus the deeds to Mrs. Rosa Thomas and to Mr. Raymond Dobyns describe the same boundary. This boundary is determined by executing a right angle off a line of the H. P. Hall survey, and proceeding to form a boundary with the land of Mrs. C. C. Chilton.

In the summer of 1912, only a few months after Mr. Downing had subdivided the Cox farm, Mrs. Rosa Thomas and her father, Mr. Louis Cox, met with Mr. Raymond Dobyns to monument the point where their properties came together. Margaret Thomas was eight and a half years old that summer. In 1973, she described the brief ceremony where her mother, her grandfather, and Mr. Dobyns buried the stone. Surveying on March 12, 1975, Mr. Charles E. Tomlin Jr., a certified land surveyor who is now deceased, observed this stone. Mr.

Tomlin fixed the position of the stone with measurements to three known, divergent objects. The measurements Mr. Tomlin gives fix the position of the stone on the N 75 E line of Mr. H. P. Hall's survey at a distance of one surveyor's chain (66 feet) from the "Small Pecan Tree" noted on Mr. Hall's survey (exhibit 2-2, page 2). This position was recovered by Mr. M. A. Wind in his survey of March 29, 2013 and by Mr. Charles R. Pruett, also a certified land surveyor, in his survey of August 19, 2014 (exhibit 6-13, page 2).

On his plat, Mr. C. E. Tomlin Jr. does not show the stone to be in the same position as his measurements fix it. Mr. Tomlin shows the stone on the northern side of the Smart family driveway while his measurements fix the stone fifteen feet southward, on the centerline extension of VSH 662. The driveway was a clear feature because it had been heavily graveled the year before Mr. Tomlin conducted his survey. From 1975 to 2013, a period of thirty-eight years, Jena and I accepted the graphically platted position for the stone. But when Mr. Michael A. Wind conducted his survey of the adjoining Dobyns property, he recovered the position of the stone fixed by Mr. Tomlin's measurements, thereby exposing the inconsistency.

It is now understood and agreed to by all parties that the stone was buried fifteen feet south of where Mr. Tomlin shows it on his plat. This fifteen-foot displacement is important because it transfers the measured and last observed position of the stone *from in line with the northern edge of the then-existing thirty foot VSH 662 right-of-way to the centerline of that road*. The N 75 E line surveyed by Mr. H. P. Hall on July 3, 1911 ran down the *center* of the old wagon road, and it was on that line the stone was buried. The stone was buried over a decade before VSH 662 was created along the course of the old wagon road.

The "Small Pecan Tree" shown by Mr. H. P. Hall on his plat at the eastern end of the N 75 E line is still living (exhibit 2-2, page 2). That "Small Pecan Tree" has grown during the last century to become a magnificent specimen over four feet in diameter. That tree bears the marks of a boundary tree made by Mr. Hall during his 1911 survey (exhibit 2-5). It is very fortunate this tree remains alive because it provides ground truth necessary to interpret Mr. Hall's survey and Mr. Downing's deeds.

From the foregoing it can be deduced that the boundary between the lands of Mrs. Rosa E. Thomas and Mr. Raymond E. Dobyns was established by three factors. First is the survey done by Mr. H. P. Hall creating the N 75 E line leading to the "Small Pecan Tree." Second are the deeds written by Mr. T. J. Downing – one to Mrs. Rosa Thomas and one to Mr. Raymond Dobyns – that specify a right angle. Third is the location where the stone was buried to determine the point where the right angle is to be turned from the N 75 E line. The boundary determined by the above factors may be obfuscated by any of three actions. The first action would be a failure to honor Mr. Hall's survey. The second action would be a failure to turn the deeded right angle. The third action would be to remove the stone. *Succeeding chapters will show that all three of those actions took place.*

During the late 1920s a drainage ditch was dug along a short portion of the boundary described by Mr. T. J. Downing between the lands he conveyed to Mrs. R. E. Thomas and to Mr. R. E. Dobyns. The year of ditch-digging is estimated by counting growth rings of trees that took root in the ditch after it was dug. The purpose of the ditch was to drain a boggy area that straddles the boundary as shown in the upper photograph of exhibit 2-6. The ditch ends when it reaches the head of a natural swale leading down to Senior Creek. During ditch digging the roots of a poplar tree growing on the west edge of the ditch were cut, but the tree was left standing and it was marked as a boundary tree. The tree survived having its roots cut, and it grew to a great size. But in the summer of 2013 this tree was taken during logging operations (exhibit 2-7, upper photo). The lower photo in exhibit 2-7 is of the boundary described by Mr. Downing. The photos in exhibit 2-7 were taken by Mr. Charles R. Pruett. In the lower photo the PVC pipe nearest to the photographer is where the stone was buried in the summer of 1912. In his survey Mr. Pruett labeled that position "Point A". The more distant PVC pipe, fifteen feet northward, indicates where the boundary line was turned in two surveys by Tomlin and Keyser, Inc.

Mr. Downing's deed to Mr. Louis Cox is found in the Lancaster County Land Records at Deed Book 58, page 140. That tract has been designated Tax Map Parcel 20-89. Mr. Downing's deed to Mrs. Rosa Thomas is found at Deed Book 59, page 359. That tract has been designated Tax Map Parcel 20-90. Mr. Downing's deed to Mr. Raymond Dobyns is found at Deed Book 58, page 119. That tract has been designated Tax Map Parcel 20-91.

Later in their lives, both Mr. Thomas J. Downing and Mr. Robert O. Norris Jr. rose to prominence in Virginia. Both Mr. Downing and Mr. Norris Jr. had bridges named after them. In 1927 the bridge across the Rappahannock River at Tappahannock was named in honor of Mr. Downing, and in 1957 the bridge across the Rappahannock River at White Stone was named in honor of Mr. Norris. Prior to the construction of these bridges, the Northern Neck was relatively isolated. Access was primarily by commercial steamboat or auto ferries. The alternative to steamboat or ferry was a rough ride down Virginia State Route 3 from Fredericksburg, Virginia. This main route jokingly came to be called "the Colonial Cow Path."

CHAPTER 3
Noah Buys Some Land

Mrs. Cornelia C. Chilton was called "Corrie" by her friends. Corrie's husband, John, passed away prior to 1912. But Corrie still owned land adjoining the Cox farm, at the time the Cox farm division took place. The sylvan beauty of old forest on what was once Corrie's land is remarkable. The land slopes downward from Sage Hill to the freshwater portion of Senior Creek. That land was designated Parcel 20-131 when tax maps were created for Lancaster County.

Earlier in their marriage, Corrie and John had owned a larger tract which extended eastward along the south side of tidal Senior Creek. But on February 21, 1874, Mr. John R. and Mrs. Cornelia C. Chilton sold 9.8 acres of their land to a freedman named Mr. Noah Tomlin Sr. Noah paid Mr. and Mrs. Chilton $148.20 for the 9.8 acres, which included about seven hundred feet of shoreline along tidal Senior Creek. That was a huge sum of money for a freedman, but gaining access to tidal Senior Creek gave Noah the opportunity to earn extra money as a part-time waterman, bringing in fish, crab, and oyster. In doing so, Noah supplemented his income from working in the fields of nearby landowners. Noah sold his catch to the buy-boat that called at the mouth of Senior Creek, and to his neighbors in the community.

Noah Tomlin recorded the deed for his purchase on March 12, 1875 at Deed Book 43, page 666 (exhibit 3-1). Interestingly, the date of his recording is one hundred years to the day before Mr. C. E. Tomlin Jr. certified a survey on March 12, 1975 that took four acres of Noah's purchase and certified it as part of Parcel 20-90 – the portion of the Cox farm that had been deeded to Mrs. Rosa Thomas by Mr. T. J. Downing.

Before he passed away Noah deeded the 9.8 acres he had bought to his son, Moton Tomlin Sr. Moton followed in his father's footsteps as a waterman and farm helper. Moton built a small home on the highest point of the land his father gave to him. That home site afforded cool breezes in the summer and a broad view overlooking Senior Creek and the land to the north. In their home overlooking the creek, Moton and his wife raised two daughters, Ada and Mary Euline. On October 9, 1911, Moton had two deeds prepared by which he divided his 9.8 acres between Ada and Mary Euline. In the first deed Moton conveyed four acres to Ada. The small home that Moton had built stood on the four acres he conveyed to Ada. In the second deed he conveyed the remainder of the 9.8 acres, or 5.8 acres, to Mary Euline. Mary Euline's land was west of Ada's land, and it encompassed an area of environmentally beautiful marsh, where tidewater and fresh water meet.

In his deed to Ada, Moton reserved the right to live out his days in the home he had built. Ada lived with her father and took care of him. It is said that Ada had been involved in "domestic difficulties" with her husband, Mr. Jackson, and Ada had injured him. Following this encounter Mr. Jackson left the area, and it was arranged that Ada would live with and care for her father. But it was understood in the community that Moton watched over Ada as much as Ada watched over him. The description for the land Moton conveyed to Ada is as follows:

> *"Commencing at the center of Seenius (sic) Creek with the land of L. O. Cox, thence in a southwesterly*

*direction along with the land of L. O. Cox to a large
white oak tree east of the house, thence along with
the same land to a holly tree marked as a corner line,
thence in a westerly direction along with the land of the
late John R. Chilton two hundred and ten yards to a
cedar stob, thence in a northerly direction to the center
of the said creek, thence down the center of the creek to
the beginning point."*

Ada's deed was recorded at Deed Book 58, page 213, on July 3, 1912
(exhibit 3-2). The "large white oak tree" mentioned in the deed
had developed heart rot and was felled during Hurricane Isabel in
September 2003. But the lower portion of its huge trunk still stands
due east of where the ruins of Moton's house stood until I removed
the building's fallen timbers and brownstone corner foundations in
1979.

On the same day Moton had the deed prepared for Ada, he also had
the deed prepared for her sister, Mary Euline. Mary Euline's deed was
recorded at Deed Book 61, page 502, on March 3, 1919 (exhibit 3-3).
The deeded description for Mary Euline's land is:

*"Commencing at a cedar stob at the corner of Ada
Jackson's land, thence in a westerly direction along with
the land of John R. Chilton, deceased, to the center of a
swamp to the land of Richmond Coleman, thence down
the center of the said swamp to the center of head of
Seenius (sic) Creek, thence down the center of the said
creek to the land of Ada Jackson, thence in a southerly
direction to the said cedar stob at the beginning point,
the same being the remainder of the tract of land of the
said Moton Tomlin, Sr. after deeding Ada Jackson nee
Tomlin four acres of his home place, which was deeded
to him by his father, the late Noah Tomlin, Sr."*

On August 16, 1971, Mr. Charles E. Tomlin Jr., who was no relation to Mr. Moton Tomlin, certified a survey of the 5.8 acres conveyed to Mary Euline by her father on October 9, 1911 (exhibit 4-1). Mr. C. E. Tomlin Jr. failed to survey the other four acres owned by the heirs of Moton Tomlin. Instead he showed that acreage to be part of Parcel 20-90. Parcel 20-90 was owned at that time by Mrs. Margaret Thomas Mallory, the daughter of Mrs. Rosa E. Thomas. Mary Euline's deed is clear that the land owned by her sister, Ada, adjoins hers to the east. Mr. C. E. Tomlin Jr. had to have read Mary Euline's deed in order to produce the survey for 5.8 acres that he certified. It is difficult to imagine how an experienced land surveyor could make such a mistake in the face of recorded deeds with good descriptions. The placement of Ada's land onto Parcel 20-90 made it seem as if her four acres had been part of the old Cox farm. But it is clear from the record that Ada's four acres and Mary Euline's 5.8 acres came from the 9.8 acres purchased by Noah from John and Corrie Chilton, and the Chilton land had never been part of the Cox farm.

Mrs. Corrie C. Chilton retained the land to the west of the land she and her husband sold to Mr. Noah Tomlin in 1874, and Noah passed the land he had bought from the Chiltons to his son, Moton. So it is that on April 30, 1912 when Special Commissioner T. J. Downing was subdividing the Cox farm, he wrote the deed to Mrs. Rosa Thomas giving the following description for the northern boundary of that conveyance:

> *"On the north by the lands of Moton Tomlin and lands*
> *of Mrs. C. C. Chilton."*

It is clear from the deed Mr. T. J. Downing wrote to Mrs. Rosa Thomas that her land and Corrie's land (now Parcels 20-90 and 20-131, respectively) share a boundary. It is interesting that while Moton had prepared the deeds to his daughters on October 9, 1911 neither Ada nor Mary Euline had recorded their deeds prior to the time Mr. T. J. Downing wrote the deeds to divide the Cox farm. That explains why Mr. Downing described Rosa's land as being bounded on the north by the lands of Moton Tomlin, and not by the lands of Ada Jackson nee Tomlin and Mary Euline Jones nee Tomlin.

After Mr. Moton Tomlin's two deeds to his daughters and Mr. Thomas J. Downing's three deeds dividing the Cox farm were recorded, a "quiet of estates" settled over the area for more than half a century. But this tranquility began to erode when Mr. Charles E. Tomlin Jr. commenced surveying land described in those deeds.

CHAPTER 4
Another Veteran Returns From War

Prior to World War II much of Southeast Asia was under French control in an area called French Indochina. During World War II, French Indochina was occupied by the Japanese. After the war the French tried to reestablish their hegemony in the area, but their efforts were abandoned after French forces were defeated by communist forces at Dien Bien Phu on May 7, 1954.

Eight years after the French defeat at Dien Bien Phu, I entered the U. S. Naval Academy in June 1962 as an eighteen year old plebe. Being young and preoccupied with my duties, I gave no thought to the consequences of the earlier French defeat. But my father, Colonel Donald V. Smart, U.S. Army, was deeply involved in those consequences. In 1962 he was serving as U.S. military attaché to Laos, which had been part of French Indochina. During his tenure in Laos, my father sent encrypted messages to the Defense Intelligence Agency regarding the shipment of arms through the southern Laotian highlands, from North Vietnam into South Vietnam. Those arms shipments violated the first Geneva Accord on Indochina, reached on July 21, 1954, by circumventing the demilitarized zone between North and South Vietnam established under the accord. The arms shipments supported the communist Viet Cong guerillas who sought to overthrow the government of the Republic of Vietnam in the south. The national command authority asked my father for more detailed information. After meeting with Miao tribal leaders and observing firsthand, my father confirmed the arms shipments along what later came to be called the Ho Chi Minh Trail.

My brother, Neil A. Smart, graduated from the U. S. Naval Academy in June 1963. By the time I graduated three years later, in June 1966, both Neil and I knew that we were destined to spend time in Vietnam. After my graduation, I was assigned to the guided missile frigate USS *Reeves* (DLG-24). During much of my two years aboard *Reeves*, the ship was stationed off the coast of North Vietnam. *Reeves'* duties were to provide tactical aid to navigation (TACAN) for U. S. aircraft flying over North Vietnam, to identify airborne enemy aircraft (IFF), to rescue downed U. S. pilots when possible, and to tally nationality and estimate tonnage of shipping entering and leaving the enemy port of Haiphong. My assignment to *Reeves* ended in mid-1968.

By 1968 my father had retired from the U. S. Army. Following his retirement, my father took an administrative position with Fairfax County Public Schools in Virginia. During that period my parents resided in Arlington County, Virginia, but they had also bought a summer vacation home in Lancaster County, Virginia. Their summer home was in a newly created waterfront community called Corrotoman By The Bay ("CBTB"). Their summer house faced south, with a beautiful view across tidal Senior Creek. That view is of the 9.8 acres Mr. Noah Tomlin Sr. purchased from John and Corrie Chilton in 1874.

After completing my tour of duty on *Reeves*, I detached from the ship in Yokosuka, Japan and returned to the United States. I spent my extended leave period between duty stations visiting my parents. During this visit my father asked me to help him build an addition onto their summer house. That sounded like great fun and I readily agreed. It turned out to be a wonderful decision. Working with my dad and sitting down each evening to dine with my parents was just the rest and relaxation that I needed. My mother was an excellent cook. I believe no one has ever made fried okra better than hers. During this vacation I became enchanted with the natural beauty of Lancaster County. Before leaving for my next duty station, I told my parents that I would like to buy some land in the area.

My second assignment was to USS *Galveston* (CLG-3), that had just been reactivated for service in Vietnam. *Galveston* was a World War II-era light cruiser that had been deactivated following that war. Prior to reactivation she was fitted with Talos guided missiles aft. She retained her two original gun turrets forward. The six barrels of those six-inch bore guns could each send ninety pound projectiles of high explosive, or variable-time fuse fragmentation, or phosphorous incendiary miles inland. The Talos missiles suppressed the North Vietnamese Air Force, and the guns supported coastal operations. I was assigned as officer-in-charge of gun Turret Two.

My tour on *Galveston* ended in mid-1970, and I returned home again. I asked my parents if we could go back to the summer house. Early one morning, soon after arriving there, my dad awakened me to say I should dress quickly and come down to our pier on Senior Creek. I did so. When I arrived, my dad introduced me to an elderly black gentleman named Welford Jones Sr. Mr. Jones stood in an open boat, holding fast to our pier.

After pleasantries, Welford asked me if I was the one looking to buy some land. I answered that I was. Welford's response astounded me. He pointed directly across Senior Creek and said, "My kin and I own about ten acres over there, and we're looking to sell." He was pointing across the creek to the land I had gazed upon while hammering, sawing, and falling in love with Lancaster County in 1968. I had carried the image of that natural beauty in my mind during days of gunfire support in the heat and noise of Turret Two. I asked Welford if he would take me across the creek in his boat to show me the land,

and he agreed to do so. It turned out to be a very enjoyable morning. In the next few hours I discovered that Welford was a wonderful raconteur of family and local history. Disembarking at an old boat landing, in an area covered with oyster shells, Welford and I pushed our way through dense mountain laurel up a steep hill.

As we walked, Welford told of his mother, Mary Euline; of his grandfather, Moton; and of his aunt, Ada. When he was a boy, Welford used to love the occasions when his mother would let him spend the day with his grandfather and with his aunt. Welford especially loved it when Moton would take him out in his small boat to go fishing or crabbing, or to tong oysters in the creek. When we reached the top of the hill, Welford paused to show me the ruins of a small house. He said that Moton and Ada had lived there before they passed away. The fallen timbers of the old house were located about twenty feet from the edge of a sharp drop-off to Senior Creek. From the edge of the drop-off, I could look down and across the creek at my parents' summer house. The old Tomlin home site was untended and the area had reverted to young forest. Several small fruit trees had been shaded out. Leaving Moton's home site, we continued westward down a more gradual hill along an overgrown road toward the freshwater portion of Senior Creek. On the way, Welford pointed out the spring where he had fetched water for his Grandfather Moton and his Aunt Ada. That spring still flows with cool, clear water.

At the end of the walk, I told Mr. Jones that I would like to buy his family's land if we could come to an agreement. I advised him that I would soon be leaving for my next duty station. I got Welford's telephone number and asked if he would coordinate with my dad and with his kin to complete the sale. He agreed to do so. Just before leaving a few days later, I called Welford. He said that he had contacted his kin and all were in agreement to sell. We settled on a price for ten acres, and I wrote a personal check for the agreed amount and left it with my dad.

After I left, my dad contacted Mr. Ray Johnston, an attorney with Clarke and Johnston, Counselors-at-Law, in Lively, Virginia. Mr. Johnston advised my father to have a survey done of the property. My father selected Tomlin and Keyser, Incorporated (T&K, Inc.) to do the survey. Mr. Charles E. Tomlin Jr. of T&K, Inc. completed the survey and certified it on August 16, 1971 (exhibit 4-1). After receiving the survey, Mr. Johnston used it to write the deed of conveyance. The deed and the survey are recorded at Deed Book 167, page 548.

After I completed my obligated service with the U. S. Navy, I transferred my commission from the U.S. Navy to the U.S. Coast and Geodetic Survey (USC&GS). My first assignment with the USC&GS was to newly commissioned Ocean Survey Ship *Researcher* (OSS-03), home ported in Miami, Florida. On the day Mr. C. E. Tomlin Jr. certified his survey, I was at sea conducting a current study in the Yucatan Channel, between Cuba and Mexico. Determining the temperature and volume of water entering the Gulf of Mexico was important to scientists developing general circulation models. When *Researcher* returned to Miami, Florida, in early December, 1971, I telephoned my parents to let them know that I was back in the United States and would be home for Christmas. During that call my father told me that my purchase of the land had closed.

While I was home for Christmas, my father and I drove from Arlington County to Lancaster County to shut off water in the summer house. I took the opportunity to record my deed and survey in the courthouse on December 20, 1971. I did not realize at the time I recorded the deed and survey that while I was at sea Mr. C. E. Tomlin Jr. had placed four acres of land owned by the heirs of Moton Tomlin Sr. onto an adjoining tract. There is no documentation to support Mr. C. E. Tomlin's addition of those separately deeded four acres to Parcel 20-90. But there are three deeds on record that indicate the four acres are not part of Parcel 20-90. Mr. C. E. Tomlin Jr. must have read those deeds. Here is why that is so.

Noah's 1874 deed states that he purchased "nine and four-fifths" (9.8) acres (exhibit 3-1). Ada's 1911 deed states that she got four acres of the 9.8 acres (exhibit 3-2). And Mary Euline's 1911 deed states she got "3 acres by estimation, let it be more or less," but the same deed goes on to describe the conveyance as "the same being the remainder of the tract of land of the said Moton Tomlin, Sr., after deeding Ada Jackson nee Tomlin four acres of his home place, which was deeded to him by his father, the late Noah Tomlin, Sr." (exhibit 3-3). Mr. C. E. Tomlin Jr. certified Mary Euline's land as 5.8 acres, which is the "remainder" of 9.8 acres minus 4 acres. Mr. C. E. Tomlin Jr. could only have known to certify 5.8 acres by reading all three deeds.

Ada's and Mary Euline's parcels, in existence since 1911, were not placed on the tax maps when those maps were created decades later. Also, when I recorded my purchase on December 20, 1971, the Commissioner of the Revenue should have designated the land I recorded as Parcel 20-131B to indicate the land had been subdivided from Parcel 20-131. Instead, the deed and survey I recorded generated a designation as Parcel 20-90A. According to a protocol in existence at the time, this designation made it appear those 5.8 acres had been subdivided from Parcel 20-90. This made it appear that my purchase had been taken from land that was once part of the Cox farm. However, it is clear from deeds on record when I recorded my survey that those 5.8 acres were never part of the Cox farm.

In June 1972 I began my first shore assignment after six years of sea duty following graduation from Annapolis. I was assigned to the International Field Year for the Great Lakes (IFYGL), with U. S. headquarters in Rockville, Maryland. The National Oceanic and Atmospheric Administration (NOAA) had just been created, and the USC&GS had become part of NOAA. At its creation, NOAA assumed responsibility for the Great Lakes survey from the U. S. Army Corps of Engineers. The Saint Lawrence Seaway had been opened in 1959, and with that opening came renewed interest in nautical charting and water quality for the Great Lakes. Canada and the United States shared this interest, and IFYGL was a great opportunity for international cooperation.

While assigned to the IFYGL Project, I was able to take some vacations. During one vacation I visited with my parents in Lancaster County, Virginia. On a pretty day I took Mr. C. E. Tomlin's plat in hand and crossed the creek to locate the monuments he had placed on the ground. I was astonished to discover that the ruins of Moton Tomlin's small house were not located on the land Mr. C. E. Tomlin Jr. had surveyed. Instead, the home site shown to me by Mr. Welford Jones was indicated on Mr. C. E. Tomlin's plat to be part of Parcel 20-90, owned by Mrs. Margaret Thomas Mallory (exhibit 4-1 - "*MALLORY*"). I was very disconcerted by this, but events were to take place within the year that seemed to resolve the matter. By an amazing bit of luck, or as I now believe by the guiding hand of Mrs. Margaret Mallory herself, I wound up purchasing her land in 1973.

CHAPTER 5
How Do I Get to My Land

After my purchase from Mr. Welford Jones and his kin, I faced the problem of access to my land, other than by boat. Mr. C. E. Tomlin's survey shows a right-of-way onto the property at the northwest corner (exhibit 4-1). Indeed, there had been a road from the black community on the north side of Senior Creek, coming from the end of what is now Sullavans Road (VSH 665) onto the Tomlin property. That long-abandoned road had crossed Senior Creek from the north just above tidewater and gone up the hill and past the spring to Moton's home. There is evidence of grading for that road on the approach to the creek, but storm waters had long ago cut through the roadbed on the flood plain of Senior Creek. It was clear to me that improving the old road from the north to permit using motorized vehicles would be very expensive. For that reason, I began looking to the south, which offered a route across high, flat land from the end of Sage Hill Road. To the north lay marsh, to the east lay tidal Senior Creek, and to the west lay rough terrain on Parcel 20-131. It was clear the best choice for a road to my land was from the south.

I saw from the Lancaster County tax map that I needed to talk to the owner of Parcel 20-90 if I wished to gain easement from the south. The tax records indicated that a woman named Margaret Thomas

Mallory owned that land. Mrs. Mallory lived at 5465 Richmond Road in Warsaw, Virginia. I resolved to visit Mrs. Mallory on my way back to work in Rockville, Maryland following a weekend at the summer house with my parents. I telephoned Mrs. Mallory to ask if I could visit. She said she would be happy to meet with me. Meeting Mrs. Mallory is one of the most auspicious events of my life. Margaret was absolutely charming. She served delicious cookies and iced tea every time I visited! On my first visit we fell into easy conversation. As Margaret learned of my love for the area where she had grown up she was delighted to tell me stories from her youth. Her recollections were vivid, and I listened with genuine fascination as she told of people and events in her community during the early 1900s. At one point Mrs. Mallory mentioned Mr. Moton Tomlin as a neighbor who had sometimes helped her grandfather with farm work. I then mentioned my puzzlement over the location of Moton's home, because a survey had been done that showed his home site to be located on her land. I could see her confusion as I described this. Seeing the look on her face, I began to fear that I might have jeopardized the purpose of my visit - to ask for easement. But in her typically gracious manner Margaret soon recovered her demeanor and shifted the conversation. At the end of my visit Mrs. Mallory stated that my request for easement would likely be no problem. However, she said that she first wished to talk to her niece, who owned a one-third share of Parcel 20-90. She asked me to call first and to stop by again in a week or two. As I left Margaret's home in Warsaw, Virginia, to drive another two hours to work in Rockville, Maryland, I felt good about my chance for gaining a right-of-way from the end of VSH 662 to the land I had bought from Welford Jones and his kin. Margaret never let on that she was seriously ill.

Margaret was seven years old when her Grandmother Elnora Biscoe Cox passed away. She was fourteen when her Grandfather Louis Oscar Cox passed away. It was evident from her conversation that Margaret loved her parents and grandparents very much. Indeed, Margaret's conversation always told of love not only for her family, but for the entire community where she grew up.

In due course I called Mrs. Mallory again, as she had requested. Early in my second visit, Mrs. Mallory told me she had talked with her niece, Mrs. Olga Dillard Novak (nicknamed "Bunnie"), and they had agreed that it was best not to encumber the value of the property by granting an easement. My heart began to sink! But before it could sink too far, Margaret went on to say that she and Bunnie had agreed to sell the entire property to me if I was interested. I almost jumped out of my seat! I know that my excitement must have shown, but it was immediately tempered by concerns over whether I could afford to buy her land. When I asked about the purchase price, Mrs. Mallory politely deferred an answer. Instead, she told me about a lifetime friend of hers named Mr. Downman McCarty, who lived in a big white house in Mollusk owned by the Stoneham Family. That house is now the Jacksonville Hunt Club on River Road (VSH 354). She said, "Please go see Mr. McCarty and walk the property with him; we'll talk price when you come again."

Again responding to Mrs. Mallory's bidding, I called Mr. McCarty and made arrangements to meet with him. On the appointed day, I stopped by the Stoneham house to pick up Mr. McCarty and we drove to the end of VSH 662 on Sage Hill. From there we began our walk into the woods. Mr. McCarty walked with a crutch because he had been wounded in World War II. Despite his handicap, he set a remarkably fast pace as we walked into the woods from the end of the public road. Within a few hundred feet we came to the head of a deep ravine. Angling left, northward, we walked along the edge of the ravine for some distance before heading down a more gradual decline to a sizable flat area. After crossing the flat area, the woods gave way to a broad and magnificent view of tidal Senior Creek looking to the east. I saw immediately that the flat area was a beautiful building site. As we headed back up the hill, Mr. McCarty commented that the land fronting Senior Creek to the north was owned by another family. I told him about my earlier purchase from Mr. Welford Jones and how that had led me to visit Mrs. Mallory. He nodded his head in understanding, and we kept walking up the hill. At the top of the hill, we walked across a larger flat area of pine forest as we angled back to the end of VSH 662. At no time during our walk did Mr. McCarty indicate any boundary lines, but at the end of our walk, I was made to understand that the route we had followed was entirely on land owned by Mrs. Mallory. I was very pleased to see that her land had a wonderful building site and that at least half of it appeared to be flat land at two different elevations.

After our walk, I drove Mr. McCarty back to the Stoneham house and returned to my parents' summer home. When I got there, I told my father what I had seen and heard. My father and I agreed that if I bought Mrs. Mallory's property, the question posed by Mr. C. E. Tomlin's 1971 survey would not be important. Following the discussion with my dad, and after buying Mrs. Mallory's property, the error in Mr. C. E. Tomlin's August 16, 1971 survey receded to the back of my mind.

After my walk with Mr. McCarty, I again called and visited Mrs. Mallory as she had asked. Early in my third visit, Mrs. Mallory gave me her asking price. I was amazed that her request was far less than what I had expected. Junior officers were not highly paid before the all-volunteer force came into being, but I had saved and invested most of my earnings during six years of sea duty as a single man. When I immediately accepted her offer, Mrs. Mallory showed obvious pleasure. She knew by our conversations that I truly loved her land, and I believe she wanted me to have it. She said that she would have the papers drawn up by her attorney, Mr. W. Tayloe Murphy. With our business concluded, we returned to talk of yesteryear.

Margaret was born on January 31, 1904. She spoke about changes on the Northern Neck following World War I, when automobiles and mechanized farm equipment began to appear. She commented that initially such equipment was too expensive for most people, and machinery did not immediately replace draft animals. The roads were rough and few outsiders visited the Northern Neck. Most trips outside the Neck were to Baltimore or Norfolk by steamboat. Those trips were well planned and often were for medical reasons. Travelers left carrying shopping lists for their neighbors. At the end of this visit Mrs. Mallory said she would contact me when the papers were drawn up, and she would ask me to stop by again. I really looked forward to my next visit.

Early in my fourth visit with Mrs. Mallory, she asked a question that surprised me. She sought reassurance that I was not buying her land for development or quick resale. I answered earnestly that I cherished the land and intended to build a home on it and to reside there when I retired from the service. She understood that my retirement was years away, for I was only twenty-nine years of age, and I had told her how much I loved my career. But I sensed that Mrs. Mallory really wanted my assurance. She went on to say that since our last meeting, she had received a telephone call from an adjoining land owner. Margaret identified the caller as a woman she knew, and she stated that this woman had offered her considerably more for her property than she was asking from me. Once again my heart began to sink until Mrs. Mallory stated forthrightly, "But I will not sell to her in any event; I will honor our agreement." Conversations with Mrs. Mallory were always interesting.

In our conversations Mrs. Mallory had spoken of the Dobyns family, who owned the land to the west, adjoining her grandfather's old farm. There were several boys in the Dobyns family. All of them were quite a bit older than Margaret. But she especially remembered Raymond E. Dobyns, who was born on October 3, 1886. Raymond was seventeen years old when Margaret was born. Raymond was just twenty-five years old, and still single, when he purchased half of her grandfather's farm in 1912. Margaret was eight years old when that sale occurred. In 1919 Raymond Dobyns married Miss Jennie Mae Towles. Margaret described Raymond and Jennie Mae as "good people." On June 5, 1921 Jennie Mae gave birth to a girl, whom they named Lorena. Lorena Dobyns was seventeen years old when her father died on April 10, 1939 from injuries he sustained in a collision between his car and a delivery truck. After Raymond Sr. died, Jennie Mae managed their estate for thirty-five years until she passed away on September 21, 1974. After her father died, Lorena went to college, and she married Mr. Marion Conner. In September 1944, Lorena gave birth to a daughter, whom they named Anita. Anita Conner was sixteen years old when her father passed away on July 31, 1961. In June 1966 Anita married Mr. Norman Tadlock. Mr. Tadlock's career took the couple throughout the world for many years.

After Jennie Mae died, Lorena became co-owner of the R. E. Dobyns estate, together with her brother Raymond E. Dobyns Jr. Lorena became the principal manager of the estate and carried those duties for the next thirty-six years, until she passed away on January 25, 2011. When Lorena passed away, her daughter, Mrs. Anita Conner Tadlock, became owner of her mother's share of the Dobyns estate. Anita and her uncle Raymond E. Dobyns Jr., formed Dobyns Family Limited Liability Corporation (Dobyns Family LLC). Anita assumed management of the corporation when it began operation on January 10, 2013.

Mrs. Lorena Conner is the one who called Mrs. Mallory in April 1973, asking to buy Margaret's land. I believe Mrs. Conner may have learned of the imminent sale of Parcel 20-90 through her position as Commissioner of the Revenue for Lancaster County. Lorena dealt with paperwork related to taxes when properties were changing ownership. Because both Mrs. Conner and Mrs. Mallory have passed away, it is unlikely that details of their telephone conversation will ever be known. But I have wondered for years why Mrs. Mallory turned down a higher offer in order to sell her land to me. I believe the land where she grew up meant something special to Mrs. Mallory and she chose to sell it to someone who evidenced the same love for the land that she felt (exhibit 5-1).

Toward the end of our fifth meeting, Mrs. Mallory brought up a new subject. She said, "Mr. Smart, when you first came to see me, you asked for an easement to other land that you had bought." In an apologetic manner she went on to say, "I must tell you that even with the purchase of my land now, you still will not have access all the way to the public road." She explained this as another bit of history.

In the summer of 1912, when she was eight and a half years old, Margaret attended with her parents a small gathering near her Grandfather Cox's house. The purpose of the gathering was for all to witness the burial of a stone marking the point where, following the subdivision of her grandfather's farm, the land that her grandfather retained, the land that her mother and father had kept, and the land purchased by Mr. Raymond Dobyns all came together. The meeting was quickly concluded because the burial point had been agreed upon and marked in advance. Years later, when the state acquired property for VSH 662, it stopped acquisition in front of her grandfather's house. The end of state road acquisition was about two hundred feet short of where the stone was buried. That explained why her land did not go all the way to the road. She stated her regret for the inconvenience, but she advised me to go see a man named Mr. Stanley Bartlett, who lived at the end of VSH 662. I was told to mention her name and to ask Mr. Bartlett for easement onto her land.

My purchase of Mrs. Mallory's land was settled on June 22, 1973. My deed was recorded at Deed Book 177, page 282, on June 25, 1973. Shortly after buying Mrs. Mallory's land, I was promoted to the rank of lieutenant commander. Thereafter, my career often required me to be away from Virginia for long periods of time. I acted quickly on the information that Mrs. Mallory had given to me to complete access to the public road. I also visited all my new neighbors. On Mrs. Mallory's advice, Mr. Stanley Bartlett and his wife, Joyce, were the first neighbors I visited. They proved to be very gracious, and sold to me a right-of-way. After that purchase I contacted T&K, Inc. to conduct a survey of the small right-of-way. Mr. Warren R. Keyser completed the right of way survey on July 13, 1973. The plat shows that Mr. Keyser found the corner stone on the northern edge of the right-of-way he surveyed, and in straight line with the *northern edge* of VSH 662 (exhibit 5-3). Interestingly, Mr. Keyser does not show the boundary between Dobyns and Smart land departing from the stone he located at a right angle to the N 75°30′00″ E line he surveyed. I recorded the deed and survey for the right-of-way on March 22, 1974. It is found at Deed Book 181, Page 490. My right-of-way was designated Tax Map Parcel 20-89A by the Commissioner of the Revenue.

In mid-June 1974 I departed for five months duty in Dakar, Senegal. Shortly before I left, I called Mrs. Mallory to thank her for all she had done for me. I am very glad that I made that call because it was my last opportunity to talk with her. While I was in Africa, Margaret passed away on July 4, 1974. She is buried at St. John's Episcopal Church in Warsaw, Virginia. Over the years I have stopped by her grave several times, and I have explained to my family how much we owe to her.

In Dakar, Senegal I was part of a United Nations, World Meteorological Organization field study. As hot, dry air flows west off the Sahara Desert, it often develops cyclonic rotation. This rotation often strengthens to storm force which may continue development to hurricane force. In the early 1970s scientists dreamed of better forecasting the growth and course of these storms. Over the years, with the use of better meteorological data, increased computing power, and continuing corrections to mathematical circulation models, remarkable progress has been made in forecasting. Improvements continue to be made, but improved forecasts have already saved many lives and much property.

I was overjoyed to return to the United States in early November, 1974 because there were even bigger things in my life than science and career. I was in love! The object of my affection was a brown-eyed, sweet-tempered, twenty-four year-old beauty named Jena Ann Beckman. I had met Jena six months before I departed for Africa.

During my stay in Africa I wrote to Jena almost every day. To my delight, she wrote back. Soon after my return from Africa, Jena and I joined my parents for a weekend at their summer house on Senior Creek. On a beautiful morning that weekend I took Jena across the creek by rowboat. We landed where Welford Jones and I had landed four and one half years earlier. Standing on a point overlooking Senior Creek, I asked Jena if she would marry me. I was overjoyed by her answer! We have named that point "Proposal Point." Jena and I were married on April 26, 1975, at Fort Myer Post Chapel in Arlington, Virginia. At the reception, my mother said: "Bob, you have married an angel." My mother was always wise and loving, and time has proven her correct.

CHAPTER 6
I Thought I Had a Road

"You shall not remove your neighbor's landmark, which the men of old have set, in your inheritance which you will inherit in the land that the Lord your God is giving you to possess."

Deuteronomy 19:14, NKJV

Prior to my departure for Senegal in June 1974, I visited each of my new neighbors. The purpose of these visits was to introduce myself and, because Mrs. Mallory's land had never been surveyed, to ask about surveys my neighbors held that would help me to learn of boundaries for my recent purchase. As mentioned, my first visit, on the advice of Mrs. Mallory, was to the Bartlett family to ask for a right-of-way. Of course the Bartlett family knew about the 1911 survey of their land (Parcel 20-89) done by Mr. Herbert P. Hall. That survey established the southern boundary of my purchase. In the course of the conversation I also learned that the Bartlett family had not asked Mrs. Mallory if they could buy her land.

My second visit was to Mrs. Dorothy W. Gardner who was listed as owner of Parcel 20-86 that adjoined Parcel 20-90 to the east. Mr. and

Mrs. Gardner lived south of Tappahannock, Virginia, on Route 17. Dorothy was very helpful, directing me to her husband, Mr. W. Rush Gardner Jr., at Gardner Realty, Inc. with office in Tappahannock. She called her husband's office to let him know I was coming. Before leaving Mrs. Gardner I mentioned that I had recently purchased my land from a woman named Mrs. Margaret Mallory. I asked if she knew Margaret or had recently spoken with her. Mrs. Gardner responded that she did not know her and had never spoken with her. By the time I arrived at Gardner Realty, Mr. Gardner had made a copy for me of a survey done in December 1919 by Mr. F. A. George (exhibit 6-1). This survey was recorded at Deed Book 62, page 246. Please note there is a line on this survey showing a boundary between the lands of Mr. Ned Thomas and Mr. Charles M. Beane on bearing S 27 ¾ W. This line corroborates the S 27 ½ W line of Mr. Hall's 1911 survey (exhibit 2-2, p. 2). Field checking, I discovered a fallen barbed wire fence still visible along the Hall and the George survey lines, as well as a marked holly tree. As a result of the Hall and the George surveys and by field evidence, I knew that the eastern and southern boundaries of my new purchase were determined by survey.

My third visit was to Ms. Helen M. Stoneham, who lived in Kilmarnock, Virginia. Helen was also very helpful. Her parents had owned two large buildings, a general store and a packing house, which stood across River Road (VSH 354) from their large home in Mollusk, Virginia. Helen told me that when her mother, Mrs. Lucy D. Stoneham, had passed away, her estate contained a number of properties in the area, but she did not know a lot about them. I was interested in Parcel 20-131, which had boundary with the property I had purchased from Welford Jones and his kin as well as boundary with the property I had purchased from Margaret Mallory. Together we searched through a box of old papers and found a survey of unknown date and origin. It seemed of interest, so I made a tracing of it. When Jena and I visited Mr. Michael Wind at his office in Tappahannock, Virginia many years later, Mr. Wind possessed a photocopy of this same survey. He was kind to make another copy of it for us (exhibit 6-2). This survey is more important than I realized in 1974. It shows the land to the east is owned by "Addie Jackson," and the land to the southeast is owned by "Heirs of Mrs. Cox." This can be no other than the land owned by Mrs. C. C. Chilton in 1912, which has since been designated Parcel 20-131. This paper confirms that the boundary between Parcels 20-90 and 20-131, which is described in the deed Mr. T. J. Downing wrote to Mrs. Rosa Thomas, was recognized and honored in the past. When I asked Helen about any recent communication she might have had with Mrs. Margaret Mallory, her answer surprised me. Helen was a young girl when Margaret was born and she enjoyed visiting the Thomas home just a few hundred yards down the road to watch baby Margaret. But she added that she had not seen or talked to Margaret in years.

After talking with the Bartletts, who owned property to the south and east; the Gardners, who owned property to the east; and Ms. Stoneham, who owned property to the north, I still needed to find out about the western boundary. That took me to the home of Mrs. Jennie Mae Towles Dobyns, the owner of record for the land to the west - Parcel 20-91. Jennie Mae lived in a beautiful home overlooking the Rappahannock River in Monaskon, Virginia. When I arrived, Mrs. Lorena Conner answered the door. I recognized Mrs. Conner from my visits to Lancaster Court House, where I had reviewed the tax maps and obtained addresses for land owners. Still, seeing her surprised me because I had not realized that Lorena Conner was a Dobyns family member. When I introduced myself as the new owner of Parcel 20-90, Mrs. Conner expressed awareness that I had purchased that land. That was not a surprise because I reasoned that as Commissioner of the Revenue she must have handled tax entries related to my purchase of Margaret Mallory's land the previous year. To my question about a land survey of Parcel 20-91, Mrs. Conner responded that no survey had been done. When I asked if she knew Mrs. Mallory, Lorena responded that she knew her and they sometimes spoke. Prior to my visit I had come to think that Jennie Mae was the woman referred to by Mrs. Mallory who had asked to purchase her land. I came to this conclusion through the process of elimination. Jennie Mae was the last owner of land adjoining Margaret's land that I visited. Lorena's statement made me think that perhaps it was her and not Jennie Mae who had called Margaret. I confirmed this later in a last conversation with Margaret. Lorena and I spoke only briefly at the door and I never got to meet Mrs. Jennie Mae Dobyns, who passed away a few months later on September 21, 1974 while I was in Senegal.

Lorena and her brother, Mr. Raymond E. Dobyns Jr., became co-owners of Parcel 20-91 after Jennie Mae's death. A few years later Lorena and her brother inherited from their uncle, Mr. Thomas A. Dobyns, Parcel 20-98 which adjoins Parcel 20-91. Lorena came to act as manager for these properties. Lorena soon asked a tenant friend of Mr. T. A. Dobyns to remove his mobile home from Parcel 20-98. She also had the original Dobyns family home on Parcel 20-98 razed and burned. Finally, she had a hedgerow along the eastern boundary of Parcel 20-98, bordering with Parcel 20-91, removed. These actions were good land management as they created one large field, making the use of large agricultural equipment more efficient. However, destruction of the hedgerow obscured the boundary between Parcels 20-98 and 20-91 that had been surveyed on January 17, 1951 by Mr. T. H. Warner (exhibit 6-3).

Shortly after the Bartlett family sold to me a right-of-way from the end of VSH 662 to the southwest corner of my land, I had that small area surveyed. The survey shows the northern edge of my right-of-way as a straight line extending from the northern edge of VSH 662, on bearing N 75°30'00" E (exhibit 5-3). This straight line is shown passing through Northern Neck Electric Cooperative (NNEC) power pole R2-229-7L and continuing straight to the corner stone that Mr. Warren R. Keyser located. Mr. Keyser measured the distance from the power pole to the stone as 215.00 feet. After I returned from Senegal, my father and I cleared the brush and small trees from our right-of-way, using Mr. W. R. Keyser's survey as our guide. When we reached the point 215 feet from the power pole and in line with the northern edge of VSH 662, we searched for the stone that Mr. W. R. Keyser had located the previous year. My father and I probed carefully along the line and then for a few feet to either side of the line. But despite much effort we did not find the stone. Thereafter, my father hired Theodore Fisher and Sons, Inc. to spread 10.45 tons of gravel down the centerline of what Mr. Keyser's survey showed to be our twenty-two foot wide right-of-way.

Two years after Mr. Keyser did the survey of the right-of-way, his corporate partner, Mr. Charles E. Tomlin Jr., was hired by the Smart family to conduct a survey of Parcel 20-90 (exhibit 6-4). In that survey Mr. C. E. Tomlin Jr. also located the southwest corner stone, but he found it in a different location from where his partner had found it. Mr. C. E. Tomlin Jr. fixed the position of the stone by means of three distance measurements and two divergent bearings to three known monuments. Geometrically speaking, Mr. C. E. Tomlin's determination of position for the stone is superior to Mr. Keyser's determination, which is based on a single bearing and a single distance to one known monument - the power pole. The measurements given by Mr. Tomlin to fix the stone are: 1) stone to power pole R2-229-7L at 179.60 feet (no bearing given); 2) stone to a pipe set by Mr. C. E. Tomlin Jr. at 128.51 feet (bearing given); and 3) stone to a tree selected by Mr. Tomlin at 751.47 feet (bearing given). Please note that Mr. Tomlin's measurement from stone to power pole is 179.60 feet, while Mr. Keyser's measurement from stone to power pole is 215.00 feet. This is an inconsistency of 35.4 feet. In May 2013 I called NNEC for information on the history of power pole R2-229-7L. I was informed that the pole had been set in 1971, two years before Mr. Keyser's survey, and it had not been replaced. In June 2016, NNEC replaced all the poles on the Sage Hill Road power line. During their work, I asked the NNEC crew to replace power pole R2-229-7L in the exact same position as the old pole. I set temporary witness marks and took photographs as the crew carefully set the new pole in the exact same location as the old pole. The new pole now bears identification number 233558. I saved the old aluminum tag (R2-229-7L) as a souvenir.

In July 1975, a few months after our wedding, Jena and I vacationed with my parents at their CBTB summer house. During that vacation my father and I took Mr. C. E. Tomlin's survey of March 12, 1975 into the field to locate the stone he showed on that plat. Our earlier efforts to locate the stone using Mr. Keyser's survey had not been successful and we felt certain that the 35.4-foot inconsistency in measurement between Mr. Keyser's and Mr. Tomlin's surveys explained why. We hoped for better results this time. In our new search we probed the ground on a radius of 179.60 feet from the power pole, and we probed the ground on a radius of 128.51 feet from the pipe Mr. Tomlin had set. For the second time my father and I could not find the stone.

Both Mr. Keyser and Mr. Tomlin showed on their plats that the stone was located on the *northern* side of our driveway, so we felt confident that our driveway was laid out correctly even though we could not find the stone. We understood from both surveys that our driveway was laid out south of the stone, on land I had bought from the Bartlett family. Mr. C. E. Tomlin Jr. could not have mistaken our driveway because my father had spread over ten tons of gravel on it about one-half year before he conducted his survey. But when Mr. Michael A. Wind conducted his survey in March 2013 he discovered that the position determined by Mr. C. E. Tomlin's three distance measurements fixed the position of the stone *south* of our driveway, not north of it. My father and I had never measured the 751.47 feet southward from the black gum tree, so it was not until Mr. Wind's survey in the spring of 2013 that I understood Mr. Tomlin's measurements fixed the position of the stone *south* of our driveway while his plat showed the stone *north* of our driveway.

Virginia minimum survey standards require that a visible monument be placed at turning points on a boundary survey. But Mr. C. E. Tomlin Jr. left no monument at the point where he turned the boundary between Parcels 20-90 and 20-91. I believe that Mr. Tomlin's measurements accurately fixed the position of the stone. But I believe that Mr. Tomlin then removed the stone and showed the position of the stone on his plat to be fifteen feet north of where the stone had been. I believe Mr. Tomlin did this for two reasons. First, by showing the turning point on the north side of our driveway, my father and I continued to accept as correct the driveway we had laid out on the basis of his partner's right-of-way survey. Second, repositioning the turning point facilitated alteration of the geometry at the southwest corner of Parcel 20-90. This helped Mr. C. E. Tomlin Jr. to draw an arbitrary western boundary for Parcel 20-90.

The original geometry at the southwest corner had been established by three factors: first, Mr. Herbert P. Hall's N 75 E line, from his survey of July 3, 1911, running to the "Small Pecan Tree"; second, Mr. T. J. Downing's description of a right angle to form the boundary between the conveyances he wrote to Mrs. Rosa E. Thomas and to Mr. Raymond E. Dobyns; and third, the location of the stone on the N 75 E line establishing the point where the right angle was to be turned. The alteration of geometry took advantage of a "swinging" effect shown graphically in exhibit 6-5. This had the effect of "swinging" the boundary eastward. To achieve the alteration of geometry, Mr. Tomlin abandoned the N 75 E line of Mr. Hall's survey; he abandoned the pecan tree at the end of that line used as an inflection point by Mr. Hall; and he abandoned the position of the stone that he had fixed by measurements. Instead, he set an ersatz monument (a section of pipe) 62.51 feet eastward of the pecan tree to serve as a new inflection point. The location for setting this pipe was carefully determined. If a circle of radius 179.60 feet is drawn centered on the power pole and another circle of radius 128.51 feet is drawn centered on the pipe, the two circles have two intersections. The northern intersection is in line with the *northern edge* of the old thirty-foot-wide VSH 662 right-of-way. This is the point where Mr. C. E. Tomlin Jr. turned the boundary line, and where he graphically indicates the stone to be located. The southern intersection lies on the extended *centerline* of VSH 662. The centerline of VSH 662 is the N 75 E line surveyed by Mr. Hall and it was on this line that Mr. C. E. Tomlin fixed by measurements the position of the stone.

Moving northward along his "swung" boundary line, Mr. C. E. Tomlin Jr. encountered a large tree he identifies as a black gum tree. The tree stood 32.4 feet east of the deeded boundary. At this tree Mr. C. E. Tomlin Jr. began a series of inflections to bend the line more sharply eastward. In doing this, Mr. C. E. Tomlin follows a line shown on the tax map. The boundary so drawn joins at the southwest corner of Parcel 20-90A. Mr. Tomlin had established that southwest corner for Parcel 20-90A in a survey he conducted on August 16, 1971 of the land I was purchasing from Mr. Welford Jones and his kin. In drawing the western boundary for Parcel 20-90 as he did, Mr. Tomlin did not turn a right angle from the N 75 E line at the stone he had located and he did not create a boundary with Parcel 20-131. Thus the boundary drawn by Mr. C. E. Tomlin Jr. is inconsistent in two major ways with the source deed for the property he was surveying.

After drawing an undocumented western boundary, Mr. Tomlin produced a surveyor's report. In this report Mr. Tomlin states: "West line as shown to me by Mr. Smart." There are problems with that statement. The first problem is that I could not have demonstrated any line to Mr. C. E. Tomlin Jr. because my NOAA fleet inspection duties did not permit me to be present in Lancaster County near the time Mr. C. E. Tomlin Jr. did his survey. Perhaps Mr. Tomlin was referring to my father in his surveyor's report. But Mr. Tomlin labeled his plat a "Boundary Survey of the Land of Robert V. Smart." Perhaps Mr. Tomlin did not know that my father's name is Donald V. Smart. Nonetheless I do not believe that my father showed Mr. C. E. Tomlin Jr. the line that Mr. Tomlin certified. If my father did show him that line, he never mentioned it to me during the remaining twenty-one years of his life. Regardless of such uncertainty, it should make no difference whether my father or I demonstrated that line to Mr. C. E. Tomlin Jr. because no demonstration can supersede a deeded description. The Virginia Supreme Court made that clear in 1921 when it ruled: *"No mere parol agreement to establish a boundary and thus exclude from the operation of a deed land embraced therein can divest, change or effect the legal rights of the parties growing out of the deed itself"* [Bradshaw v. Booth, 129 Va. 19, 105 S. E. 555, 1921].

I believe Mr. Tomlin should have followed the deeded description for the western boundary of Parcel 20-90. He did not do so. I believe Mr. Tomlin falsified his surveyor's report in an attempt to substantiate an arbitrary boundary line he knew was inconsistent with the deed. And I believe Mr. Tomlin removed the stone and left no monumentation at the southwest corner of Parcel 20-90.

On January 6, 1988 Mr. T. W. Rhodes, an engineer with the Virginia Department of Transportation, did a survey at the end of VSH 662 to create a school bus turn- around area (exhibit 6-6). This survey is recorded at Deed Book 278, page 371, and it shows the *northern edge* of the Smart family driveway in line with the *northern edge* of VSH 662, passing through the power pole. Mr. Rhodes's survey gave my father and me further assurance that our driveway was laid out correctly.

Soon after I retired in June 1996, Jena and I wished to remodel the house my parents had built twenty years earlier. In order to obtain a building permit, we had to have another survey done of Parcel 20-90. Again we hired T&K, Inc., to do the work. Mr. Warren R. Keyser conducted this survey and certified it on May 28, 1997 (exhibits 6-7 and 6-8). During this survey Mr. Keyser did not find the stone that he had found on July 13, 1973. Nor did he find the stone that his partner, Mr. C. E. Tomlin Jr., had found on March 12, 1975. Because he could not find the stone, Mr. Keyser set a rod at the point where he turned the western boundary line. Mr. Keyser set this rod in line with the *northern edge* of the old thirty foot wide right-of-way for VSH 662, which he labeled VSH 622 (exhibit 6-8). Mr. Keyser gives the entering bearing to the rod he set as S 72°58'20" W. This is the same bearing by which Mr. Tomlin arrived at the stone from the pipe he had set. Mr. Keyser gives the departing bearing from the rod he set as N 10°58'26" W. This is the same bearing on which Mr. Tomlin departed the stone. The distances given by Mr. Tomlin and Mr. Keyser on those bearings are also identical. With identical bearings and distances to the same two objects (pipe and tree) Mr. Keyser perforce had to have set the rod at the same location where Mr. Tomlin found the stone. I accepted this for an additional sixteen years until Mr. Wind reestablished the true position for the stone and set the corner stake at that position - *south of our driveway.*

After a few days of field work following Mr. Wind's placement of his corner stake, I discovered that his placement was correct. This discovery was amazing to me. But along with that discovery I made another discovery. By using a protractor on exhibit 6-8 it can be seen that Mr. Keyser *graphically* drew a true right angle (90°) at the southwest corner of his survey. But by calculation of the angle between Mr. Keyser's entering and departing bearings at the southwest corner, it can be determined that Mr. Keyser did not turn the right angle he draws on his plat. He followed Mr. C. E. Tomlin's survey by turning an angle of 83°56'46". The *graphical* presentation of a right angle gives to the observer an impression of compliance with the description in the deed. But the truth is otherwise.

When I became aware of the inconsistency between the calculated angle and the graphically displayed angle, I knew something was amiss. Both Mr. Tomlin and Mr. Keyser very likely read the source deed for the land they were surveying. That deed calls for turning a right angle at the southwest corner, yet both surveyors failed to turn a right angle. Why was it drawn as a right angle?

Sixteen years before he did the survey of Parcel 20-90, Mr. Warren R. Keyser surveyed Parcel 20-89. Mr. Keyser certified his survey of Parcel 20-89 on February 24, 1981 (exhibit 6-9). Parcel 20-89 is the same tract surveyed by Mr. Herbert P. Hall on July 3, 1911. Because Mr. Hall and Mr. Keyser were surveying the same tract, their surveys should be almost identical. But they are not. The two surveys differ because Mr. Keyser took distance measurements from the ersatz monument (pipe) that his partner, Mr. C. E. Tomlin Jr., set in March 1975. Of course, Mr. Hall took his measurements from the "Small Pecan Tree." Because Mr. C. E. Tomlin Jr. set the pipe 62.51 feet eastward from the pecan tree, Mr. Keyser's measurements using the pipe are shifted 62.51 feet eastward. I believe Mr. Keyser recognized there was a problem. I believe that is why he made the following annotation on his plat: "Note: North and west lines not surveyed by me." The north and west lines not surveyed by Mr. Keyser represent about 60 percent of the total boundary for what he labels a "Boundary Survey of the Land of Stanley B. Bartlett." Since he did not close a boundary survey of Parcel 20-89, Mr. Keyser should not have certified acreage. Nevertheless, he certifies Parcel 20-89 to contain 21.326 acres. This is over half an acre more than the twenty and three-quarter acres determined by Mr. H. P. Hall. If Mr. Keyser had identified the Hall pecan tree during his survey in 1981, he would have resolved his problems in surveying Parcel 20-89. He might also have resolved problems that he encountered sixteen years later when he surveyed Parcel 20-90. Mr. Hall's survey had been on record since May 18, 1912 at Deed Book 58, page 140. And the pecan tree noted on Mr. Hall's survey had not moved. It was a lost opportunity to correct Mr. C. E. Tomlin's survey of March 12, 1975 before other events added complexity to the situation.

The "Small Pecan Tree" shown on Mr. Hall's survey has grown to be a large tree since 1911. Unfortunately, that tree was not recognized by three certified land surveyors. First, there was Mr. C. E. Tomlin Jr., in 1975; second, there was Mr. W. R. Keyser in 1981 and again in 1997; and third, there was Mr. M. A. Wind in 2013. Fortunately, Mr. Charles R. Pruett identified the pecan tree in his survey of August 19, 2014 (exhibit 6-13, pages 1 and 2). In his survey Mr. C. R. Pruett drew the boundary between Parcels 20-90 and 20-91 according to the description given by Mr. T. J. Downing. He labeled this boundary as Line "A-F." Mr. Pruett determined Line "A-F" by turning a right angle off the centerline of VSH 662 at the point where Mr. C. E. Tomlin Jr. found the stone. This position for the stone was recovered by Mr. M. A. Wind. The centerline bearing for VSH 662 used by Mr. Pruett was determined by Mr. M. A. Wind in his survey of March 29, 2013. Thus, Line "A-F" is the boundary described by Mr. T. J. Downing and executed based on parameters determined by Mr. Wind.

A few weeks after I began my research, I called Mr. Wind to ask if Jena and I could meet with him. Mr. Wind agreed and we met in his office in Tappahannock, Virginia on May 7, 2013. At that meeting Jena and I asked Mr. Wind to show on his plat the boundary described in Mr. T. J. Downing's deed to Mrs. Rosa Thomas. Mr. Wind declined to show that line on his plat. Before departing, Jena and I requested that Mr. Wind show on his plat *both* the Downing Line and the Tomlin Line. Mr. Wind declined this request as well.

Some time later the following was given in pre-trial disclosure material: *"Mr. Wind's court house research uncovered a deed to the original owner of Mr. Smart's property which is recorded in Deed Book 59, at page 359. The language in this deed concerning the western boundary of this tract has some language that could be argued to conflict with the two plats prepared for and recorded by the Smarts."* From that material I believe it is reasonable to conclude there is an inconsistency between the western boundary described at Deed Book 59, page 359 and the two plats prepared for and recorded by me. Virginia Code 18VAC10-20-370 gives the following guidance for handling inconsistencies found while conducting a survey:

> *"The professional shall clearly identify on the plats, maps, and reports inconsistencies found in the research of common boundaries between the land being surveyed and the adjoining land(s)."*

I believe Mr. Wind should have shown both the Downing Line and the Tomlin Line on his plat.

About a week after our visit with Mr. Wind on May 7, 2013, Jena and I received a letter dated May 10, 2013, from Mrs. Anita Conner Tadlock, Manager of Dobyns Family LLC. In this letter Mrs. Tadlock advised Jena and me that she intended to file Mr. Wind's survey "no later than May 13, 2013." The letter went on to state: "We have signed a contract for timber harvesting on the entire Dobyns Family LLC tract, and we understand initial cutting could be imminent, but likely would not occur within two weeks." (exhibit 6-14). Mrs. Tadlock's letter took Jena and me by surprise. After more than a week of thought, Jena and I sent a letter to Mrs. Tadlock, dated May 21, 2013, which we hoped would explain our thinking and which we hoped would be taken as friendly in tone (exhibit 6-15, pages 1-4). Mrs. Tadlock's response to our letter confirmed her corporation's previously stated intent to proceed with logging (exhibit 6-16). Jena and I were uncertain how to handle this. We believed then and still believe that Mr. Downing's description in the deed he wrote to Mrs. Thomas is quite clear. In addition, we were becoming concerned about the implications this dispute had for the deed we received from Mrs. Mallory. We decided the time had come to seek legal counsel. We were advised by counsel to assert our claim in writing and to advise Mrs. Tadlock of penalties for logging across boundaries. I drafted the letter and mailed it on June 1, 2013 (exhibit 6-17).

I was young in 1973 when the Bartlett family sold a right-of-way to me. I believed then that I had resolved the problem of access to my property. I thought I had a road, and so it seemed for forty years - from 1973 to 2013. During those years multiple surveys were conducted and every survey led Jena and me to believe that our driveway was laid out correctly. For forty years the Smart family had driven openly, exclusively, and continuously over land we believed we owned through purchase from the Bartlett family. We had made improvements to this land, and we had maintained it. Not once were my parents, nor Jena and I, questioned by Mrs. Lorena Dobyns Conner about our use of a fifteen foot wide strip of her land as part of our driveway.

Our use of that driveway came to an end on Thursday, December 4, 2014 when Dobyns Family LLC had a fence constructed to block our driveway. The top photo in exhibit 5-2 shows the corner of the completed fence. The strip of exposed gravel between the first and second fence posts in that photo shows the course of our old driveway. The white PVC pipe with blue survey tape tied to it marks the spot where the stone was buried in the summer of 1912. The bottom photo of exhibit 5-2 shows the location of the old Cox family home. The one story portion of the house seen in the photo was built in the 1940s on the same footprint as the original home of Louis O. and Elnora B. Cox.

The morning of fence construction Jena and I got telephone calls from two neighbors telling us of the work being done at the entrance to our property. I went in haste to the entrance. Upon arrival I asked that construction be stopped. Mr. and Mrs. Tadlock were present at the scene. They declined to order a stop to construction, so I returned home and called the Lancaster County sheriff's office which sent a deputy to the scene. The Tadlocks showed the deputy a copy of the court decree from the trial that had taken place on September 11, 2014, so the deputy could not intervene. Copies of my T&K, Inc. surveys were as useless as my deed had been at trial! The court decree stated that the line surveyed by Mr. Wind was the true boundary. Jena and I had agreed even before the trial that Mr. Wind's determination for the southwest corner of our land, where the PVC pipe stands in the photo, was correct (exhibit 5-2). So, as I cooled down a bit, I realized that we could not stop the building of the fence despite my three T&K, Inc. surveys and the VDOT survey which all showed our driveway layout to be correct.

The anguish caused by poorly done surveys endured. For example, over two years after the trial, on October 11, 2016, the timber standing on the area between the Downing and the Tomlin Lines was harvested. Knowing that the court decree gave ownership of that area to Dobyns Family LLC, I could only watch as the cutting progressed. It was not fun to watch the century old hardwood trees come down, and to listen to the high-pitched whine of the massive cutting machine. I understand that trees are a renewable resource, but I am old and will never again see big, beautiful trees on that land. I believe Mrs. Mallory would have felt the same sickening feeling that I did. Luckily she did not have to witness the harvest.

When the fence was completed Jena and I faced another problem. A large, leaning tree stood between the corner of the fence and the H. P. Hall pecan tree. This tree could be skirted by cars and pick-up trucks, but fire department personnel confirmed that longer and taller vehicles, such as fire trucks and propane delivery trucks, could not negotiate between the Hall pecan and the leaning tree. Again Jena and I sought legal counsel. Our attorney advised us that we could likely gain prescriptive easement to continue use of our original driveway based on our lengthy usage. But he added that the process would take time. With winter approaching, Jena and I needed a quick solution to this problem. We also were aware that even if we won prescriptive easement, we would still be driving over a small strip of land owned by Dobyns Family LLC, and we had no desire to do that. We decided not to seek prescriptive easement. But that left us with only one option.

For the second time in my life, I went to see Mrs. Joyce (Bartlett) Clarke about a right-of-way onto our property. After I explained our predicament, Joyce immediately agreed to let us move our driveway southward fifteen feet. A deed of boundary adjustment was soon signed and recorded as Instrument No. 150001348 in the Lancaster County Land Records. Joyce has been a wonderful neighbor for many decades and we truly appreciate her friendship. Acting quickly following the agreement with Joyce, I cut down the large, leaning tree and split it into firewood. I then hired Mr. Victor Lawyer, with his excavator, to remove the tree stump and to fill in the hole. Next I hired Mr. Bobby Haynie to spread three truckloads of gravel. Exhibit 6-18 shows the results of this labor. In the end, the driveway situation has worked out quite well. The total cost of moving our driveway was less than the predicted legal fees for obtaining prescriptive easement. Jena and I believe that the new driveway is superior to the old one because it is entered from the right-hand side of Sage Hill Road and because it does not run over the roots of a huge tree halfway down the driveway. That tree and the close-by tracks of the old driveway can be seen at the left edge of the photo in exhibit 6-18.

During the trial on September 11, 2014, much testimony was given regarding acreage, but my ability to hear is so bad that I could not fully understand what was being said. After Jena's and my loss at trial, my lack of understanding about what had transpired was especially unsettling. I hoped that better understanding of what had been said would help me to sleep through the night. To learn more about the trial, I contacted the transcription service company, Capitol Reporting, Inc., and I bought the trial transcript. It proved to be fascinating reading. After reading the transcript, I continued my research in the Lancaster County land records. The Clerk of the Circuit Court and her staff were very helpful in teaching me how to conduct research. Two months after the trial, in November 2014, I was researching in Deed Book 58 when I came upon Moton Tomlin's deed to his daughter Ada. This deed is found on page 213 of that book (exhibit 3-2). As I read of Moton Tomlin's love for his daughter, the words of Mr. Welford Jones, Moton's grandson, came back to me. Here was proof that Welford had told me the truth during our walk in 1970 and again when I questioned him five years later. *It became clear to me that Mr. C. E. Tomlin Jr. had conducted two surveys for the Smart family that were not carefully done, and that those surveys were the root cause of many problems.*

By the time I arrived home from the courthouse I knew that I had much more research to do. I knew that finding Ada's deed was a major breakthrough because it was proof that acreage testimony used by the plaintiff to support its acreage apportionment argument was not correct. I saw the need for new direction in my research.

One research avenue appeared to be a seeming nexus between faulty surveys and faulty tax maps. I needed to learn more about the tax maps. Specifically, did the tax maps conform to recorded deeds? Chapter 8 relates what I learned about the tax maps.

A second avenue was to learn more about what had been done in 1911. Was Mr. H. P. Hall's survey of good quality? That survey was clearly the basis for many of the boundaries arising from subdivision of the Cox farm. Yet Mr. Hall's survey had been defamed at trial. Was Mr. Hall's survey really as bad as alluded, or was it a solid foundation to carry out the agreement approved by the court on April 9, 1912? The following is what I learned about Mr. Hall's survey.

During my career with NOAA, I received training in surveying (exhibit 6-19). I bought a surveyor's transit and I asked Mrs. Joyce (Bartlett) Clarke if I could retrace the footsteps of Mr. Hall around her property. Joyce gave me permission and I spent two beautiful and fun days in the field. I felt young again!

Surveyors in 1911 had no global positioning system, no laser geodimeters, and no computers to make their work easier. They generally surveyed long, straight lines in order to more easily draft their plats and to calculate acreage. Mr. Hall almost certainly took his bearings and turned angular measurements using a telescopic brass transit with vernier scale and magnetic compass mounted on a wooden tripod. For distance measurements Mr. Hall almost certainly used a one-hundred-link steel chain that was sixty-six feet in length and made of a low coefficient of thermal expansion alloy. Mr. Hall probably began his survey at a common point, such as the pine tree at the southern apex of his survey, where the lands of Mr. Louis O. Cox, Mr. Charles M. Beane, and Belmont Farm (now Heritage Point Development) joined.

Presuming Mr. Hall started at the pine tree, he likely proceeded as follows. Setting up and leveling his transit beside the pine tree, Mr. Hall turned a 45° internal angle westward from the S 27 ½ W boundary with Mr. Beane's land. His new bearing was N 17 ½ W. Mr. Hall then measured the distance from the pine tree down the N 17 ½ W line to the *center* of the wagon road that passed in front of the Dobyns and the Cox homes. He obtained a measurement of 21.00 chains, or 1,386 feet. One hundred and two years later Mr. Wind determined a distance of 1,364.06 feet from a rod he set in the stump hole of that pine tree to the northwest corner pin for Parcel 20-89. That NW corner pin stands at the southern edge of the forty-foot wide public right-of-way for VSH 662 (exhibit 6-10). Half the right-of-way width is twenty feet. Thus, Mr. Hall's and Mr. Wind's surveys agree to within 1.94 feet. Here is how that is determined. Mr. Wind measured 1,364.06 feet from the pine stump to the southern edge of the road. When the twenty feet from the southern edge of the road to the *center* of the road is added to the 1,364.06 feet measurement, it yields 1,384.06 feet. This is 1.94 feet less than the 1,386 feet (twenty-one chains at 66 feet per chain) that Mr. Hall measured. Mr. Hall's measurement is amazingly accurate considering that he was using a heavy steel chain in rough terrain.

After moving his tripod from the pine tree to the grassy strip in the center of the wagon road, Mr. Hall leveled his transit and sighted down the centerline of the road in front of the Cox home. In his telescope Mr. Hall saw a small pecan tree in line with the centerline of the road. The pecan tree stood at the edge of the woods, about two hundred feet from the home of Mr. Louis O. Cox, and about the same distance from the head of a deep ravine. Sighting on the small pecan tree, Mr. Hall turned an internal angle of 87 ½° to obtain a new magnetic bearing of N 75 E. In 2013 Mr. Michael Wind obtained a magnetic bearing for the centerline of VSH 662 of N 76° 24' 52" E, or within 1 ½° of what Mr. Hall found. Considering the use of different compasses and changes in the earth's magnetic field over the last 102 years, the two bearings are amazingly close.

When Mr. Hall conducted his survey in 1911, there was no state road system. Mr. Louis Cox, for whom Mr. Hall was doing the survey, owned the land on both sides of the N 17 ½ W and the N 75 E lines that he had just surveyed. Mr. Hall's survey was likely done in preparation for subdividing Mr. Cox's farm. *When the subdivision occurred, based on Mr. Hall's survey, the center of the road became the northern boundary between the curtesy retention of Mr. L. O. Cox and the land he sold to Mr. R. E. Dobyns.* Only after creation of the public right-of-way for VSH 662 and after surveys by T&K, Inc. indicated the northern edge of that public right-of-way to be the boundary, did ambiguity arise as to whether the original boundary was the centerline of VSH 662 or the northern edge of the original thirty foot wide public right-of-way. However it is now clear from Mr. Hall's survey that the original boundary was the centerline of the road.

Moving his tripod from the northwest corner of the tract he was surveying, Mr. Hall reestablished his tripod astraddle the small pecan tree on the tree's north side at the eastern end of the N 75 E line. He leveled his transit and took a bearing that bent his previous N 75 E line 7 ½° to the right, in order to avoid the deep ravine. His new bearing was N 82 ½ E, and this produced an internal angle of 172 ½°. Mr. Hall measured eight chains, or 528 feet, on bearing N 82 ½ E from the pecan tree to the boundary with Mr. C. M. Beane's land. Before departing the location beside the pecan tree, Mr. Hall emblazoned the "Small Pecan Tree" with three marks on its north side to monument that tree as a turning point in the boundary. Moving his tripod from the pecan tree, Mr. Hall reestablished his tripod on the line between the lands of Mr. L. O. Cox and Mr. C. M. Beane. Mr. Hall leveled and sighted down that boundary line on bearing S 27 ½ W. This created an internal angle of 55°. Mr. Hall closed his survey at the pine tree where he had started, after measuring a distance of 27.30 chains, or 1801.8 feet, along the S 27 ½ W line.

Mr. Hall's angular closure (45°+87½°+172½°+55°=360°) is perfect. His distance measurements are remarkably accurate for chain work in rough, wooded terrain. The positions of the pine tree at the southern apex of the tract and of the pecan tree at the northern apex, as shown on his plat, are known. These positions form an axis that anchors Mr. Hall's survey. The survey's orientation on the ground is fixed and any suggested reorientation is spurious.

The answer to the question of whether Mr. Hall conducted an accurate survey is "yes". In my opinion, Mr. Hall's survey is more accurate in many respects than some other surveys done in the area using far better equipment. Mr. Hall's survey is a solid basis for subdividing Mr. Cox's farm under terms of the agreement approved by Lancaster Circuit Court on April 9, 1912.

I believe that Mr. C. E. Tomlin Jr. recognized that Mr. H. P. Hall's survey is fundamental to understanding the deeds that Mr. T. J. Downing wrote to subdivide the Cox farm. I believe that Mr. C. E. Tomlin Jr. wished to alter a boundary described by Mr. Downing. I believe Mr. C. E. Tomlin Jr. knowingly debased Mr. Hall's survey by setting an ersatz monument (pipe) in lieu of the original monument (pecan tree). I believe that the ersatz monument confused later surveyors. Not until Mr. Charles R. Pruett conducted his survey of August 19, 2014 was the pecan tree used by Mr. Hall reestablished as the true inflection point on the northern boundary of Parcel 20-89. Mr. Pruett noted that the pecan tree stood exactly one surveyor's chain from where Mr. C. E. Tomlin Jr. last saw and fixed the position of the stone.

CHAPTER 7
A Magnificent Deceit

The Beame and Chaine balke no Truthes nor blaunch Untruthes. Take away Number, Weight, Measure you exile Justice and reduce and haile-up from Hell the olde and odious Chaos of Confusion.

> William Folkingham, Feudigraphia, 1610.
> From "Surveyors and Statesmen", Sarah S.
> Hughes, The Virginia Surveyors Foundation

In 1964 my father retired from the U. S. Army, with service during World War II, the Korean Conflict, and the buildup to the Vietnam Conflict. After retirement from the army, my father went back to his pre-WWII career in education, taking a position with Fairfax County Public Schools (FCPS) in Virginia. He rose to become Assistant Superintendent of FCPS Area 1, with an enrollment of forty-one thousand students. My mother, Ocie, continued her work as a second-grade teacher with Arlington County Public Schools. By 1975, my father was ready to take a second retirement. Both he and my mother retired at the end of that school year. My mother had been teaching, off and on, since 1933. My parents now had the means to enjoy a lifestyle unimaginable to them when they eloped to Pensacola,

Florida at the height of the Depression because they had no money for a wedding. During the years they lived in Arlington County, Virginia, my parents came to love Lancaster County, Virginia where they kept the summer home.

One evening early in 1975, when my parents were making plans for their retirement, Jena and I had dinner with them at their Arlington, Virginia home. The conversation turned to the subject of suitable retirement abodes. Both my mom and dad wanted to retire in Lancaster County, but my mother had one reservation which she expressed as follows: "Don, we both love the Northern Neck, but I don't think the summer home is suitable for our retirement." My mother was not generally outspoken but when she came out like that, my dad listened.

I was doing some creative thinking after a couple of my dad's gin and tonics, and I ventured the following: "Hey Mom! Why don't you and Dad build the home you want on the land I bought across the creek?" The idea was received enthusiastically.

Being a retired army colonel, my dad was a take-charge guy and things soon began to happen. My father learned that to get a building permit a survey would have to be done of the land I had bought from Mrs. Mallory two years earlier. This would be the first survey ever done of the 1912 conveyance to Mrs. Rosa E. Thomas. As with the 1971 survey of Parcel 20-90A (a portion of Moton Tomlin's land) and the 1973 survey of Parcel 20-89A (my right-of-way), we hired T&K, Inc., to do the survey of Parcel 20-90. Mr. Charles E. Tomlin Jr. completed the work and certified his survey on March 12, 1975 (exhibit 6-4).

One hardly knows where to begin describing the many significant errors in Mr. C. E. Tomlin's survey. I guess I will start with the southern boundary and go clockwise around what Mr. Tomlin called a "Boundary Survey of the Land of Robert V. Smart." *The entire southern boundary is wrong. It does not comport at a single point with the adjoining northern boundary for Parcel 20-89 established by Mr. Herbert P. Hall in his survey for Mr. Louis O. Cox on July 3, 1911.* Mr. Hall's survey was cited by Lancaster Circuit Court in its decree on April 9, 1912, and Mr. T. J. Downing included Mr. Hall's survey as part of the first deed he wrote to divide the Cox farm. Then he used Mr. Hall's survey to define boundaries within the subdivision. Mr. C. E. Tomlin Jr. obviously saw Mr. Hall's survey, for he takes a measurement of 528 feet (eight chains) from it. But Mr. Tomlin ignored the pecan tree used by Mr. Hall at the west end of that measurement. Instead, Mr. Tomlin placed an alternative monument (pipe) 62.51 feet east of the pecan tree and took his 528.10 foot measurement from the pipe. This causes Mr. Tomlin's S 80°28′20″ W line to differ from Mr. Hall's commensurate N 82 ½ E line. Superficially, Mr. Tomlin's survey seems to share one point with Mr. Hall's survey. That is the point on Mr. Hall's N 75 E line where the stone was buried. Mr. Tomlin indicates turning the line at the stone. But in fact, Mr. Tomlin turned the western boundary for Parcel 20-90 at a point fifteen feet north of where he fixed the position of the stone. Thus, from his turning point fifteen feet north of the stone, to his arbitrarily set pipe, and then on to the boundary with Parcel 20-87, which is the entire southern boundary, Mr. C. E. Tomlin's survey does not share a single point with Mr. Hall's survey.

Continuing clockwise, the western boundary drawn by Mr. C. E. Tomlin Jr. does not comport at a single point with the deeded description for that boundary written by Mr. T. J. Downing. In his survey Mr. Tomlin gave measurements that fixed the position where he found the southwest corner stone. But then Mr. Tomlin shows on his plat that he turned the line at a position fifteen feet north of where his measurements fixed the stone. Mr. Tomlin then left no monument at the point where he turned the line, and he left no monument at the position where his measurements fixed the stone. When he turned the line to begin the western boundary, Mr. C. E. Tomlin Jr. did not turn a right angle as called for in the deed Mr. T. J. Downing wrote for Mrs. Rosa Thomas. Instead, Mr. C. E. Tomlin Jr. turned an internal angle six degrees *less* than a right angle. Proceeding north on this arbitrary line, Mr. Tomlin chose a large black gum tree as an inflection point in the boundary. The tree he chose stood 32.4 feet east of the deeded boundary. At this tree Mr. Tomlin began a series of bends that turned the line even farther eastward. In doing so he followed a line depicted on the tax map (exhibit 8-1). Mr. Tomlin's western boundary ends at the southwest corner of Parcel 20-90A. Mr. Tomlin had established that point in his survey of incorrectly designated Parcel 20-90A. In drawing the western boundary of Parcel 20-90 as he did, Mr. C. E. Tomlin Jr. ignored the description for the western boundary contained in the source deed for the land he was surveying. There is no documentation to support the line that Mr. Tomlin drew. The boundary drawn by Mr. C. E. Tomlin Jr. placed 1.842 acres of land embraced in the deed for Parcel 20-90 onto Parcel 20-91, co-owned at that time by the Commissioner of the Revenue.

Continuing clockwise, the northern boundary is almost entirely wrong. Mr. T. J. Downing's deed to Mrs. Rosa Thomas describes her conveyance as bounded: *"On the north by the lands of Moton Tomlin and the lands of Mrs. C. C. Chilton."* But Mr. C. E. Tomlin's survey fails to produce a boundary with the land owned by Mrs. C. C. Chilton in 1912. By the time Mr. C. E. Tomlin did his survey in 1975, the Chilton land (Parcel 20-131) was in the estate of Mrs. Lucy D. Stoneham. Mr. Tomlin labels the area to the northwest of the western boundary he drew as *"STONEHAM EST"* (exhibit 6-4). This label gives the impression that a boundary is created between Parcel 20-131, the land owned by Mrs. C. C. Chilton in 1912, and Parcel 20-90. I believed this to be true for thirty-eight years, but I never understood where the common point for Parcels 20-90, 20-91, and 20-131 was located because Mr. Tomlin does not show that point on his survey plat. The official tax map has never shown any boundary between Parcels 20-90 and 20-131 as described in the deed for Parcel 20-90 (exhibits 8-1 and 8-2). Not until Mr. Charles R. Pruett conducted a survey on August 19, 2014, is the common point derived by following the deeded description shown on a survey. Mr. Pruett labeled this juncture "Point F", and he labeled the line described in Mr. Downing's deed to Mrs. Rosa Thomas as Line "A-F" (exhibit 6-13, page 1).

Continuing along the northern boundary, a substantial portion of that boundary simply disappears. The missing portion of the boundary is that with the land Moton Tomlin deeded to his daughter Ada on October 9, 1911. The disappearance of the boundary with Ada's land is a result of Mr. C. E. Tomlin's incorporation of Ada's land into Parcel 20-90. The lost boundary is about seven hundred feet. Mr. C. E. Tomlin Jr. fails to give measurement across that area. By failing to either survey the shoreline of Senior Creek or to develop a tie line across that area, Mr. C. E. Tomlin Jr. fails to close a boundary survey of Parcel 20-90. Despite this failure Mr. Tomlin labels his work a "Boundary Survey of the Land of Robert V. Smart", and he certifies Parcel 20-90 to contain twenty-five acres (25.0 ac.). This statement of acreage will become crucial in the trial on September 11, 2014.

Continuing clockwise, the eastern boundary is not entirely correct. The distance of 425.19 feet given on bearing S 29° 31' 40" W is too short. This curtailment results from the fact that Mr. C. E. Tomlin Jr. took his measurement of 528.10 feet on the southern boundary from the pipe he set rather than from the pecan tree used by Mr. Hall. Taking essentially the same measurement as Mr. Hall from a point 62.51 feet east of where Mr. Hall commenced his measurement (pipe versus pecan tree) causes Mr. Tomlin to encounter the boundary with Parcel 20-87 at a different location. To accommodate the 528.10 feet measurement Mr. Tomlin took, he "slid" the juncture along the boundary with Parcel 20-87. This causes Mr. Tomlin to shorten the eastern boundary with Parcels 20-86 and 20-87. The shortened eastern boundary causes a further small reduction of area in Parcel 20-90.

The work of Mr. Tomlin in his "Boundary Survey of the Land of Robert V. Smart" is largely a product of his imagination and it has caused a great deal of confusion. He has brought up the "olde and odious Chaos of Confusion" recognized for centuries as the product of poor survey work.

The boundaries shown on his "Boundary Survey of the Land of Robert V. Smart" violate descriptions in *five* deeds on record at the time he did his survey. Those deeds are: Deed Book 58, page 119 from Mr. T. J. Downing to Mr. Raymond E. Dobyns recorded on May 1, 1912; Deed Book 58, page 140 from Mr. T. J. Downing to Mr. Louis O. Cox recorded on May 18, 1912; Deed Book 58, page 213 from Mr. Moton Tomlin to Mrs. Ada Jackson nee Tomlin recorded on July 3, 1912; Deed Book 59, page 359 from Mr. T. J. Downing to Mrs. Rosa E. Thomas recorded on April 24, 1914; and Deed Book 61, page 502 from Mr. Moton Tomlin to Mrs. Mary Euline Jones nee Tomlin recorded on March 3, 1919.

Jena and I were married in 1975 just seven weeks after Mr. C. E. Tomlin Jr. completed his survey of Parcel 20-90. Four months before our marriage, I had been assigned as NOAA Fleet Inspection Officer. This assignment kept me traveling most of the time. It was not until February 4, 1976, almost a year later, that I had a chance to record Mr. Tomlin's survey in the Lancaster County land records. I now understand how stupid it was for me to record that survey. But even as I admit that fact, I am astounded that a certified land surveyor would certify so flawed a survey. In my opinion, a plat that has been certified by a land surveyor licensed to practice in Virginia should be conducted with faithfulness, understanding, and care. In my opinion a survey certified by a land surveyor licensed to practice in Virginia should be true to deeds on record at the time the survey is conducted. In my opinion a person who pays a certified land surveyor to produce a survey should not be compelled to personally verify every mete and bound of the product, as I have very belatedly done, for fear of harm to their lawful estate. In 1705 the Virginia Legislature recognized that good survey work is fundamental to real estate transactions and holdings. It is vital to Virginia's economy that survey work is done with integrity. In my opinion, certification of a land survey by a certified land surveyor should free the recipient from the principle of *caveat emptor.*

During construction of my parent's retirement home my parents lived at their summer house in Corrotoman By The Bay. One weekend during that period Jena and I stayed with them. Early one morning during that weekend I saw Mr. Welford Jones coming up Senior Creek in his boat. I walked down to the pier to greet him. During our conversation I mentioned my confusion over his grandfather's home site. I told him that a survey of his family's land had been done in 1971 and that this survey showed his grandfather's home was located on land owned by a woman named Margaret Mallory (exhibit 4-1, *"MALLORY"*). I went on to say that in 1973 I had bought Mrs. Mallory's land, and just the previous year her land had been surveyed by the same surveyor. That survey also showed Moton's home to be located on the land we had bought from Mrs. Mallory. I recalled what he had told me during our walk almost five years earlier, and I was puzzled by why the surveyor had shown his grandfather's home site to be located on Mrs. Mallory's land.

Without fluster Welford explained that his grandfather had inherited "about ten acres" from his great grandfather. Years later his grandfather divided the land he had inherited between his mother and his Aunt Ada. After his grandfather and his Aunt Ada passed away, no one took up residence in Moton's old home, and it eventually fell into disrepair as we had seen on our walk. Welford's mother, Mary Euline, had inherited her sister's land on which the old home stood. Welford avowed that his Grandfather Moton had always gotten along well with Mr. Cox and with Mr. Thomas. He was sure there had never been a boundary dispute. Welford seemed forthright and certain of his facts. At the end of our conversation, I believed Welford was telling the truth and that Mr. C. E. Tomlin Jr. had made a mistake.

After that discussion, the matter again receded in my thinking. I reasoned that through a "mix-up" I had seemingly bought Moton's home site twice – once through my negotiations with Welford, and once from Margaret Mallory and Bunnie Novak. Only after the trial forty years later about the western boundary, that came to hinge on acreage apportionment of the old Cox farm, did I understand how important was the question of Moton's home site.

Moton was a poor and uneducated man. His father, Noah, had been a slave. Both were good men. In very difficult circumstances both Noah and Moton worked hard to achieve something and to provide for their families. They both loved their children. Moton took care to have deeds written to convey to his daughters the land that his father had given to him. In 1980 I cleared Moton's home site and built a firewood drying shed just a few feet from where that home had stood. But every year a few daffodils spring up at the edge of the drop-off in front of Moton's old home site and that causes me to think about him. As I use my hydraulic log splitter to make firewood, I think about Moton and his family. They lived with no electricity or running water, and with only the most basic hand tools to help them in their work. Noah and Moton spent their lives working on the water, or walking behind a mule to plow other people's land. I wish I could have met and talked to them. If they were like Welford Jones I think I would have liked them.

When the western boundary dispute arose, I did not see a connection between the disputed western boundary and the mystery of Moton's old home site. As we prepared for trial, our attorney, Mr. Michael L. Donner, concentrated on the deeded description for the disputed western boundary. Mr. Donner asked our expert witness, Mr. Charles R. Pruett, to do a survey of the disputed area showing the line described by Mr. T. J. Downing in his deed to Mrs. Rosa Thomas. In his survey Mr. C. R. Pruett showed both the Tomlin Line and, for the first time ever on a survey, the line described by Mr. Downing (exhibit 6-13, page 2). Mr. Pruett labeled the Downing Line as line "A-F." Point "A" is where Mr. Pruett turned the line. That is the point on the N 75 E line of Mr. Hall's survey where the stone was buried in the summer of 1912. That point had been recovered by Mr. M. A. Wind in his survey of March 29, 2013. Point "F" is the point where the boundary meets Parcel 20-131, the land owned by Mrs. C. C. Chilton in 1912. To execute the description in the deed, Mr. Pruett used the centerline for VSH 662 determined by Mr. Wind. As the turning point on that line (Point "A") Mr. Pruett used the position recovered by Mr. Wind. Finally, Mr. Donner verified there was no documentation on record to support the Tomlin Line. Jena and I thought these were strong preparations to defend our deed.

But when we got to trial, we found these preparations were not as strong as we had thought. Remarkably, from the outset of the trial Special Commissioner T. J. Downing's deeds played almost no role. The deeds were quickly relegated by talk of acreage, and all the acreage talked about was presumed applicable to the 1912 Cox Farm subdivision agreement. Jena and I were totally unprepared to counter a summary dismissal of our deed. I believe the plaintiff's argument seemed plausible to the jury because it is true the deeds dividing the Cox farm arose out of the agreement. To seal Jena's and my fate, I had recorded two T&K, Inc. surveys that showed Parcel 20-90 contained acreage in excess of the agreement's provisions for subdivision of the Cox farm.

As a result of the plaintiff's argument, the trial quickly came to hinge on acreage apportionment under the agreement. Following the trial I bought and read the trial transcript. In reading the transcript it became clear that the crux of the trial was the testimony the jury heard regarding the acreages for Parcels 20-90 and 20-91 - the parcels lying on either side of the disputed boundary. When this became clear to me, I wanted to know if there was any documentation in the Lancaster County land records to confirm what Welford Jones had told me about his grandfather's old home site. Following the trial I spent time in the Records Room going through century-old deed books. It was mid-November 2014 when I pulled Deed Book 58 from the shelf and turned to page 213 (exhibit 3-2). As I read the deed recorded on July 3, 1912, telling of Moton's gift to his beloved daughter Ada, I knew that Welford, Moton's grandson, had told me the truth. I paid the clerk to make a copy of that page and I made additional copies of it when I got home. About three weeks later, on December 4, 2014, I gave a copy of Ada's deed to Mrs. Tadlock as she and her husband were supervising construction of the fence to block Jena's and my driveway.

By the time of the bicentennial on July 4, 1976, my parents had completed their new home and moved into it. Jena and I shared in the combined festivities of the bicentennial and house warming. The following year I ended my assignment as NOAA Fleet Inspection Officer and took command of a pair of hydrographic survey ships. My command kept me away from home most of two years. Coming off this sea tour, I was promoted to the rank of commander and assigned as student at the Armed Forces Staff College in Norfolk, Virginia. On November 7, 1978 Jena gave birth to our first child, Jason. I was blessed to be present for his birth at Portsmouth Naval Hospital in Portsmouth, Virginia. On the very same day, just hours before Jason was born, his future wife, Suzanne, was born to Mr. and Mrs. Alan Rich in Cardiff, Wales of the United Kingdom. Given the timing of their births, one may conjecture the stars were in alignment for a Rich and Smart wedding! After graduation from the Staff College, I was assigned to the Office of the Secretary of Commerce for NOAA Policy and Planning. While I was stationed in Washington, DC our second child, Tamara, was born on October 29, 1981. I was blessed as well to be present for her birth at Bethesda Naval Hospital, in Bethesda, Maryland.

In 1982 I became Director of the National Ocean Service Manned Diving Program. In 1984 I was assigned as a student at the U. S. Naval War College in Newport, Rhode Island. After graduation from the War College, I was sent to sea again. This tour was on NOAA Ship *Surveyor* (OSS-03), home ported in Seattle, Washington. I saw little of Jena, Jason, and Tammy during those two years. I don't know how Jena managed all by herself to raise two young children with no grandparents nearby. Coming off *Surveyor* I was assigned as Chief, Office of NOAA Commissioned Personnel, in the Washington DC area. During that assignment I was promoted to the rank of captain.

There is an inevitable final tour of sea duty for the seagoing officer who remains in service long enough. It is jokingly called "The Twilight Cruise." My "Twilight Cruise" came with assignment as Commanding Officer of the 4,050 ton NOAA Ship *Discoverer* (OSS-02), home ported in Seattle, Washington. *Discoverer* was the largest ship active in the NOAA fleet at that time. During this assignment my family stayed in Silver Spring, Maryland because *Discoverer* was scheduled to be away from Seattle for most of the time I was aboard. Jason (then fourteen) and Tamara (then eleven) were happy to remain with their friends in Maryland. During most of the two years that I was on *Discoverer*, the ship was assigned to deploy and maintain a vast array of large, instrumented buoys. We anchored these buoys across the equatorial Pacific Ocean, often in water over three miles deep. The array, still maintained today, is 1,200 nautical miles wide, spanning from ten degrees north latitude to ten degrees south latitude, and ranging from the Galapagos Islands in the east to Indonesia in the west. The array monitors ocean current with depth, insolation, sea surface temperature, salinity and temperature with depth, wind speed and direction, and wave height over the tropical Pacific. The data is radio transmitted to the NOAA Pacific Marine Environmental Laboratory in Seattle, Washington where it is used to improve long-range extra-tropical forecasts throughout the world. During the time I was away, Jena went back to school at Montgomery College and got a degree in music.

The last assignment of my career was back in Washington, DC. My immediate boss was Dr. Ned Ostenso, the Associate Administrator for Oceanic and Atmospheric Research. Dr. Ostenso had previously been at the Office of Naval Research. My assignment was made possible by the end of the Cold War. I was assigned to help identify environmental data that had been given national security classification upon collection but that might now be declassified. This effort greatly benefited the research of environmental scientists who did not possess national security clearances, and the program proved to be a great success. For example, throughout the Cold War both the United States and the Soviet Union operated submarines in the Arctic Ocean, where they amassed huge archives of environmental data. The U.S. Naval Oceanographic Office took the lead to produce a declassified atlas of the Arctic Ocean. The Russians produced a similar atlas using data they had collected. These atlases have proved valuable to scientists studying the Arctic region. Other work involved marine mammal studies using the Navy's integrated undersea surveillance system, and efforts to declassify decades of satellite imagery in order to study trends in global biomass and global urbanization.

I loved my work with NOAA, but the Defense Officer Personnel Management Act, which governs NOAA Commissioned Officers, required that I retire on completion of thirty years commissioned service because I had not been selected for flag rank. I retired on June 1, 1996, in a ceremony at the U. S. Naval Academy. I had been in uniform for almost two-thirds of my life, since swearing- in as a plebe at the Naval Academy in 1962. The major benefit of retirement was that Jena and I could choose where we wanted to live. We soon sold our house in Montgomery County, Maryland and moved to Lancaster County, Virginia. Jena and I were excited that our dream, and my promise to Mrs. Margaret Mallory, were coming true. I especially looked forward to being closer to my parents. Unfortunately, I did not have much time with my father. On September 24, 1996, less than four months after I retired, my father passed away at eighty-four years of age. My mother continued living at Rappahannock-Westminster Canterbury, in Lancaster County, Virginia, until she passed away on May 4, 2005, at ninety-three years of age.

My parents grew up poor in Baldwin County, Alabama, near the Gulf of Mexico. Despite their lack of money, both my mom and dad obtained bachelor's degrees in education during the Depression at the University of Alabama, Tuscaloosa. To help pay education expenses, my father participated in the U.S. Army's Reserve Officer Training Program at the university. The army life appealed to him, but when he graduated in 1933, the army was not commissioning reserve officers. That was the case because the United States kept a very small standing army between World Wars I and II. However, my dad continued to attend army reserve summer training camps throughout the 1930s as a means of earning a little extra money. By December 7, 1941, my dad was principal of the high school at Victoria, Texas. When war was declared the day after the Pearl Harbor attack, my father was soon called to active duty. His years of training in infantry tactics and his experience as an educator were put to use as an instructor at the U.S. Army Infantry School in Fort Benning, Georgia. Almost every one of the second lieutenants trained at Fort Benning shipped out immediately after graduation to either the European or the Pacific theaters. When the war ended, my father decided not to return to his pre-war position as principal of the high school at Victoria. Instead, he took the examination to become a regular commissioned officer. This was when practically everyone else was mustering out of the service as fast as they could. After receiving a regular commission, my father was assigned to the staff of General Mark Clark, commanding US Occupation Forces in the American sectors of Austria and the city of Vienna. My father's main responsibility was democratizing the schools for Austrian children in the American sectors. The Great Depression and World War II clearly shaped my parent's lives. They were resilient in economic depression and in time of war. They were part of a truly great generation.

After I retired in June 1996, Jena and I decided to remodel the house my parents had built twenty years before. In order to get a building permit for remodeling, we had to have another survey done of Parcel 20-90. Again we hired T&K, Inc., to conduct the survey. Mr. Warren R. Keyser completed the work on May 28, 1997 (exhibits 6-7 and 6-8). The bearings and distances recorded by Mr. Keyser in his survey are almost identical to those of the survey conducted by his partner, Mr. C. E. Tomlin Jr., twenty-two years earlier. However, there is one major difference between the two surveys. This difference occurs at the southwest corner. Mr. Keyser was unable to find the stone that he had located in 1973 during his right-of-way survey, and that his partner had located in 1975. Unable to find the stone, Mr. Keyser set a rod where he turned the line to begin the western boundary for Parcel 20-90. He set the rod in line with the northern edge of the old thirty foot wide right-of-way for VSH 662. By the time of his survey in 1997, the state had widened the road to a forty foot wide right-of-way. Please note the detail at the southwest corner in exhibit 6-8.

Mr. Keyser's survey appeared consistent with his partner's earlier survey, and so Jena and I accepted it and recorded it. We were completely unaware that Mr. Keyser set the rod fifteen feet north of where his partner's measurements fixed the position of the southwest corner stone. Our awareness of this did not come until sixteen years later when Mr. M. A. Wind did his survey. At the point where Mr. Keyser set the rod, he graphically drafted a true right angle on his plat. But his entering and departing bearings at the rod yield a calculated angle of $83° 56' 46''$. The observer is led by the graphical presentation to think that Mr. Keyser turned a true right angle in his survey, thus honoring the deed that Mr. T. J. Downing wrote for Mrs. Rosa Thomas. Only by mathematical calculation does one realize the angle turned is six degrees less than the right angle described in the deed.

As mentioned earlier, Mr. Wind's survey in 2013 prompted me to give my T&K, Inc. surveys detailed scrutiny for the first time. I soon discovered that the western boundary surveyed by Mr. Tomlin in 1975, and followed by both Mr. Keyser and Mr. Wind, is not consistent with the description for that boundary written by Mr. T. J. Downing. Also in early field work I discovered the pecan tree that Mr. H. P. Hall had used in his survey of July 3, 1911. In stripping away the English ivy that had grown around and up the tree, I discovered the marks of a boundary tree. Shortly thereafter I discovered another tree with boundary marks. The second tree was a poplar tree with its roots cut and marks on its east side that stood on the west edge of a shallow drainage ditch. The tree was located about halfway down the deeded boundary line (exhibit 2-7, upper photo). Unfortunately this tree was cut during logging operations contracted by Dobyns Family LLC in 2013.

There is no evidence that Mr. Raymond E. Dobyns Sr. ever contested the deeded boundary between his land and the land of Mrs. Rosa Thomas. Mr. Dobyns was a party to the 1912 agreement. He was also a party to the burial of the stone. He very likely agreed to have the ditch dug because it benefited him as well as the Thomas family by draining a boggy area straddling the boundary between their properties. Unfortunately, Mr. Dobyns died at fifty-two years of age in 1939 as a result of complications following an automobile accident. After his death, his wife, Jennie Mae, managed their estate for thirty-five years. As with her husband, there is no evidence that Jennie Mae ever contested the boundary described by Mr. T. J. Downing. Jennie Mae died at seventy-nine years of age on September 21, 1974, just two and one-half months after Margaret Mallory passed away.

CHAPTER 8

Tax Map Puzzle

Tax maps were developed for Lancaster County in the middle of the last century. The tax maps were intended as a tool to aid in accounting for taxable real estate. But over the years, tax maps have also come to be used by the public for general conceptualization of land holdings. While the tax maps may have use by the public, their use in that regard must be exercised with caution. This is because courts have consistently held that tax maps are not authoritative with regard to extent or boundaries of land holdings.

Since their creation, the Lancaster County tax maps have undergone several revisions. These revisions were necessary to portray newly subdivided parcels and to correct errors in earlier editions of the maps. For example, a revision was necessary in the late 1960s to portray the newly created residential waterfront community called "Corrotoman By The Bay." While such revisions are necessary, any changes made to the tax maps must be based on documentation. Recorded deeds are the preeminent form of documentation.

The Commissioner of the Revenue is the county's chief tax assessor, and is responsible for maintaining the tax maps. The position of Commissioner of the Revenue is established by the Constitution of Virginia. This makes the Commissioner a sworn Virginia Constitutional Officer.

Mrs. Lorena Dobyns Conner served in the Lancaster County Commissioner of the Revenue Office for forty-two years. She began work there in 1953, serving first under her uncle, Mr. Ernest F. Dobyns, who began his tenure in 1943. Mrs. Conner became Deputy Commissioner of the Revenue in 1955 and became Commissioner of the Revenue in 1972. She served in that position until her retirement in 1995.

When the tax maps were created, a protocol was adopted for designating later subdivisions of land. The protocol is based on the "parent parcel" from which the subdivision was taken. For example, under the protocol, Parcel 20-131A would be the correct designation for the first recorded parcel created from land taken from Parcel 20-131. Parcel 20-131B would be the correct designation for the second recorded parcel taken from Parcel 20-131, and so forth. This protocol prevents the "creation" or "destruction" of land through administrative process.

When I bought land from the heirs of Mr. Moton Tomlin in 1971, the deeds Moton Tomlin had written to his daughters, Ada and Mary Euline, had been on record for over half a century. Their recording date was long before the Lancaster County tax maps were created. But when the tax maps were created, Ada's and Mary Euline's parcels were not given designation and were not added to the tax maps. After I recorded my purchase of Mary Euline's land in 1971, that parcel was belatedly given designation and placed on the tax map. However, it was designated incorrectly according to the protocol. The land Mary Euline had owned was designated Parcel 20-90A. This made it appear that her land had been taken from Parcel 20-90. The correct designation for Mary Euline's land should have been Parcel 20-131B. This would have reflected that her land was the second recorded subdivision taken from Parcel 20-131. Ada's land, mentioned in the deed for Mary Euline's land, remained without designation.

I beg the reader's patience to review the sequence of actions that led to effectively abolish a lawfully deeded and recorded tract. On February 21, 1874, Mr. John R. and Mrs. Cornelia C. Chilton sold nine and four-fifths (9.8) acres to Mr. Noah Tomlin Sr. Late in his life Noah conveyed those 9.8 acres to his son, Moton Tomlin Sr. On October 9, 1911, Moton deeded four of those 9.8 acres to his daughter Ada. The same day, Moton deeded the remainder of his land, or 5.8 acres, to his daughter Mary Euline. Ada recorded her deed in the Lancaster County land records on July 3, 1912. Mary Euline recorded her deed seven years later, on March 3, 1919. Several decades later, tax maps were created for Lancaster County. At that time the parcel from which Noah's purchase had been taken was designated Parcel 20-131. But the two parcels created from Noah's purchase were not given designations and were not added to the tax map.

In 1971, I bargained to purchase from the heirs of Mr. Moton Tomlin the land he had deeded to Ada and to Mary Euline. Prior to my purchase, Mr. C. E. Tomlin Jr., who was no relation to Mr. Moton Tomlin, was hired by my father to survey the land that the heirs of Moton Tomlin were selling. Mr. C. E. Tomlin Jr. surveyed only the 5.8 acres embraced in the deed to Mary Euline, and did not survey the four acres embraced in the deed to Ada. In his survey of August 16, 1971 Mr. C. E. Tomlin Jr. indicated Ada's four acres to be part of adjoining Parcel 20-90. The attorney who drafted the deed for my purchase used the metes and bounds on Mr. C. E. Tomlin's survey to write the deed of conveyance to me. Thus, by my purchase from the heirs of Mr. Moton Tomlin, I wound up with title only to the 5.8 acres embraced in the deed to Mary Euline as surveyed by Mr. C. E. Tomlin Jr. Subsequently I purchased Parcel 20-90 in 1973. Two years later Mr. C. E. Tomlin Jr. was again hired – this time to survey my 1973 land purchase. In the survey that Mr. Tomlin completed on March 12, 1975, he certified Ada's four acres to be part of Parcel 20-90.

Thus Ada's land was erased from the modern record. Her land never made it onto the tax map and now it was shown on two certified surveys, which I had accepted and recorded, as part of Parcel 20-90. The only proof of Ada's land as a separately deeded tract was the entry made on July 3, 1912 at Deed Book 58, page 213.

When I recorded my deed for Mary Euline's land on December 20, 1971, the Commissioner of the Revenue designated that land as Parcel 20-90A. The designation as Parcel 20-90A gave the appearance by the protocol that my 5.8 acres had been taken out of Parcel 20-90. But no land was actually taken from Parcel 20-90 because Mary Euline's land had never been part of that parcel. Early in 1973 the Commissioner of the Revenue attempted to purchase Parcel 20-90. But the owner of that land, Mrs. Mallory, chose to sell her land to me and not to the Commissioner. Two years later, in 1975, Mr. C. E. Tomlin added Ada's land to Parcel 20-90 in a certified survey. By doing this he actually increased the area of Parcel 20-90 because Ada's land was not previously a part of Parcel 20-90. In the same survey Mr. C. E. Tomlin Jr. drew an arbitrary western boundary for Parcel 20-90 that followed a line shown on the tax map drawn by the Commissioner. This line was inconsistent with the deeded description in the source deed for Parcel 20-90. The arbitrary and undocumented western boundary line transferred 1.842 acres embraced in the deed for Parcel 20-90 onto land co-owned by the Commissioner (exhibit 9-1). After adding four acres and subtracting 1.842 acres, and after failing to close his survey, Mr. C. E. Tomlin Jr. certified Parcel 20-90 to contain twenty-five acres. This certified acreage was crucial testimony to the jury on September 11, 2014.

Mr. T. J. Downing's deed to Mrs. Rosa Thomas describes a northern boundary with land owned by Mrs. C. C. Chilton in 1912. Later, Mrs. Chilton's land came into possession of the Stoneham Family, and that land was designated Parcel 20-131. In his survey of Parcel 20-90 on March 12, 1975, Mr. C. E. Tomlin Jr. labeled the land northwest of the arbitrary western boundary he drew as *"STONEHAM EST"* (exhibit 6-4). For many years I interpreted this label as fulfilling the description for the northern boundary given in Deed Book 59, page 359. But I never knew where that boundary began because Mr. C. E. Tomlin Jr. did not indicate the common point where Dobyns, Stoneham, and Smart lands came together. I assumed it was at the black gum tree. Years later I noticed that the tax map showed Parcel 20-91 completely separated Parcel 20-90 from Parcel 20-131 (exhibit 8-1). That meant the tax map was not consistent with *either* my deed or with Mr. C. E. Tomlin's survey. This was confusing but my confusion was about to get much worse!

In 1993 the Commissioner of the Revenue published a revision to the tax map (exhibit 8-2). In this revision the Commissioner moved Parcel 20-131 westward about a quarter of a mile. The new position for Parcel 20-131 made it impossible for Parcel 20-90 to have the boundary with Parcel 20-131 that is described in deed. In addition, the movement of Parcel 20-131 removed the boundary with Parcel 20-90A, which should have been designated Parcel 20-131B.

The movement of Parcel 20-131 created a large vacant area. Into this area, reaching all the way to the freshwater portion of Senior Creek, the Commissioner extended Parcel 20-91 that she co-owned. There is no documentation in the Lancaster County land records to support the movement of Parcel 20-131. There is also no documentation to support the extension of Parcel 20-91 into the area vacated by Parcel 20-131. But there *is* documentation to support the position of Parcel 20-131 adjoining Parcels 20-90 and 20-90A.

Please take time to compare exhibit 8-1 (pre-revision) and exhibit 8-2 (post-revision). From my research I believe I have solved the tax map puzzle. I admit that I am not a graphic artist, but exhibit 8-4 is my drawing of how the tax map should look based on Lancaster County land records. Please also take time to compare exhibit 8-2 and exhibit 8-4.

When Jena and I visited Mr. Michael A. Wind in his office on May 7, 2013, he kindly gave us a copy of an old drawing with the words

"Heirs of Mrs. Cox" handwritten on its southeast corner (exhibit 6-2). I had made a tracing of this drawing during my visit with Ms. Helen Stoneham in 1974, but at that time I failed to appreciate its significance. The drawing is of Parcel 20-131, and the label "Heirs of Mrs. Cox" shows that a boundary between Parcel 20-131 and Parcel 20-90 was understood and honored in the past.

During the trial on September 11, 2014, the manager of Dobyns Family LLC testified the tax map shows the boundary between Parcels 20-90 and 20-91 bends to go down a swale. Indeed the tax map shows such a bend. But the tax map line eliminates the boundary between Parcels 20-90 and 20-131 that is described in Mr. Downing's deed to Mrs. Thomas. The tax map is not an authority to establish new boundaries. The tax map should have been drawn as described in the deed. Mr. C. E. Tomlin Jr. followed the tax map. He should have drawn the line described in the deed. After following the tax map, Mr. C. E. Tomlin Jr. labeled the land to the northwest of that line as property of the "*STONEHAM EST*". That label obscures the fact that the line he drew is inconsistent with the deed in that it does not create a boundary with Parcel 20-131. In his survey of March 29, 2013 Mr. Michael A. Wind also followed the tax map line. But Mr. Wind labeled the land to the northwest of that line as property of Dobyns Family LLC (exhibit 6-11). I was completely confused. According to the tax map and certified surveys, properties were changing position and changing ownership with no documentation.

In his 2013 survey, Mr. M. A. Wind "returned" Parcel 20-131 to its documented position. It was correct that he did so. But why did the movement of Parcel 20-131 not pique his curiosity as to other inconsistencies? Here is a bit of dialogue from a deposition that Mr. Wind gave three weeks before the trial. In this passage, Jena's and my attorney, Mr. Michael L. Donner Sr., questions Mr. Michael A. Wind:

Q Did you say that you had reviewed the tax maps in Lancaster County as well?

A I have, yes.

Q Okay. And what tax maps did you review?

A I reviewed every - I guess every issue of them, if you will, from - I think the first one was done in 1947 up until today. There are, I want to say, four or five revisions along the way, maybe half a dozen revisions.

Q What is the - what was the tax map designation for Mr. Smart's property, the boundary of which is at issue here, do you know?

A Section No. 20, Parcel 90.

Q Okay. And what is the tax map designation for the parcel that's owned by the plaintiff?

A The parcel adjoins Mr. Smart is tax map 20-91.

Q Okay. Did you notice any change in the parcel designated 20-91 between 1970 and 1998?

A Yes.

Q Okay. And did you ask any questions as to why it had changed?

A I knew why it changed.

Q Why did it change?

A It changed because of other surveys that had been done.

Q Let me show you - I don't have this marked as an exhibit but perhaps I will. I'm going to show you an unmarked exhibit right now. Let your counsel look at that as well. Do you see the change in there between the mid `70s and 1998 in tax map 91?

A Yes.

Q Okay. And do you see how tax map 131 has been moved to the west and tax map 90A has been changed so that tax map 91 now goes all the way to the top of the page?
A Yes.

Q And your testimony is that that's simply a surveying error?
A No, that's when - 90A was changed when Charlie Tomlin surveyed it, and that was about the same time in the '70s. And so once they had that survey, they modified the tax map and they had to do something with the other land. And they just drew 91 up there for lack of anything better to do I guess.

Q Okay. So when you say that they drew 91 up there for lack of anything better to do, doesn't that indicate something that should pique your interest as to why that was changed other than just something better to do?
A Well, I knew why it was changed. Why they chose to put 91 up there instead of moving 131 over, I didn't know that, but that really doesn't bother me, no.

On March 29, 2013 Mr. Wind certified a survey in which he brought Parcel 20-131 back to its correct position (exhibit 6-11). In doing this he squeezed Parcel 20-91 out of its extruded area and established a boundary between Parcels 20-91 and 20-131. On a straight portion of that boundary Mr. Wind set a cedar stob near what would be the common point for Parcels 20-90, 20-91, and 20-131 if the boundary described in the deed by Mr. T. J. Downing to Mrs. Rosa Thomas was executed based on Mr. H. P. Hall's survey (exhibit 6-12, lower photo). In a survey which he certified on August 19, 2014 Mr. C. R. Pruett labeled Point "F" as the common point for Parcels 20-90, 20-91, and 20-131 (exhibit 6-13, page 1). Mr. Pruett turned a right angle from bearing N 76° 24' 52" E. This is the centerline bearing for VSH 662 determined by Mr. Wind. Mr. Pruett turned that angle at the turning point recovered by Mr. Wind. Mr. Pruett labeled that position, where the stone was last seen, as Point "A". Thus, Mr. Pruett drew Line "A-F" as the line described in Mr. Downing's deed, based on Mr. Wind's survey. Mr. Pruett's "Point F" and Mr. Wind's cedar stob are 58.29 feet apart.

Mr. H. P. Hall developed a bearing of N 75 E down the centerline of the old wagon road and Mr. M. A. Wind developed a bearing of N 76°24'52″ E down the centerline of VSH 662. This is a difference of 1°24'52″. Over the 1,144.19 feet length of Line "A-F" Mr. Pruett's "Point F" would move 28.25 feet closer to Mr. Wind's stob if Mr. Pruett had turned the deeded right angle from Mr. Hall's N 75 E bearing. We do not know exactly why Mr. Wind placed a cedar stob on a straight line, but it is very interesting that Mr. Wind's cedar stob and Mr. Pruett's "Point F" are so close together.

Here is another interesting question. Mr. Wind acknowledged reading Deed Book 59, page 359 that describes a right angle and a boundary with Mrs. Chilton's land. In his survey Mr. Wind determined all the parameters required to draw the deeded western boundary of Parcel 20-90. Mr. Pruett used the information determined by Mr. Wind to draw the deeded boundary on his plat. Why did Mr. Wind refuse to use the information he had derived in order to draw the deeded boundary on his own plat? I believe that 18VAC10-20-370 required him to do so.

While the Commissioner of the Revenue seems to have given great thought to the northern end of the Downing Line, she failed to correct an error at the southern end of that line. The failure at the southern end has to do with the tax map depiction of the land retained by Mr. Louis Oscar Cox when he subdivided his farm. That land was designated Parcel 20-89 when the tax maps were developed. On April 30, 1912 Mr. T. J. Downing included, as part of the first deed he wrote to subdivide the Cox farm, a copy of the survey done by Mr. Herbert P. Hall of the land that became Parcel 20-89 (exhibit 2-2, page 2). That survey shows a basically *triangular* tract. But the tax map shows Parcel 20-89 as a *quadrilateral* tract (exhibit 8-3). Over a period of twenty-two years, the Commissioner of the Revenue added three subdivisions to the tax map for land taken from Parcel 20-89. Those subdivisions are Parcels 20-89A, 89B, and 89C. Each of those entries required close examination of Parcel 20-89. Mrs. Conner was quite familiar with the area, where her family owned land and near where she grew up. But during three close inspections of Parcel 20-89 the Commissioner failed to correct the erroneous depiction.

The erroneous depiction of Parcel 20-89 eliminates the N 75 E line surveyed by Mr. H. P. Hall in 1911. That is the line on which the cornerstone was buried in 1912. The cornerstone was seen and fixed on that line by Mr. C. E. Tomlin Jr. on March 12, 1975. Then the cornerstone disappeared. The pecan tree used by Mr. Herbert P. Hall on July 3, 1911 stands at the eastern end of the N 75 E line. That pecan tree went unrecognized by Mr. C. E. Tomlin Jr. and two other later surveyors. Not until August 19, 2014 was the tree again identified, when Mr. Charles R. Pruett found it where Mr. Hall showed it to be – at the eastern end of the N 75 E line. It is very fortunate Mr. T. J. Downing included a copy of Mr. Hall's survey with the deed he wrote to Mr. Louis Oscar Cox. And it is fortunate that Mr. Downing personally recorded that deed with the survey on May 18, 1912 (exhibit 2-2). If not for Mr. Downing's assiduous efforts, recognition of the N 75 E line of Mr. Hall's survey would probably have been lost.

I believe there were consistent efforts made to obfuscate Mr. Hall's survey. Mr. Hall's survey is essential to interpret the deeds that Mr. T. J. Downing wrote. In the deed Mr. Downing wrote to Mrs. Thomas, he writes: "... *said westward boundary is to run at right angles to the line of the land of the said L. O. Cox as same has heretofore been surveyed and for that purpose reference is hereby made to the plat of said Coxes land made by H. P. Hall dated July 3, 1911 and of record with the deed of said L. O. Cox.*" That statement is meaningless without the information contained in Mr. Hall's survey.

The renderings on the tax map in the area of study for this book are to a great extent inconsistent with land records. Here are examples of how documentation and the tax map differ. The tract described in Ada's recorded deed never received designation and was never added to the tax map. The tract described in Mary Euline's deed received designation and was added to the tax map only after I recorded the deed for my land purchase from Mr. Welford Jones and his kin in 1971. But that tract was then given an incorrect designation that confused its true origin. Twenty-two years later, Parcel 20-131, the "parent parcel" of Ada's and Mary Euline's land, was moved westward without documentation. Then Parcel 20-91, co-owned by the Commissioner, was extended without documentation into the area vacated by Parcel 20-131. Parcel 20-89 remained incorrectly depicted. And finally, the boundary between Parcels 20-90 and 20-91 remained incorrectly drawn through several revisions. The incorrect depiction transferred land embraced in the deed for Parcel 20-90 onto land co-owned by the Commissioner.

Upon creation of the waterfront communities of "CBTB" and "Heritage Point", the total assessed value of individual building lots greatly exceeded the original value of the acreage. I am sure Mrs. Mallory understood the potential monetary gain to be realized by creating a residential waterfront community similar to nearby "CBTB" and Heritage Point. But Mrs. Mallory loved the land her parents had bought from her grandfather and where she had grown up. I believe that as Mrs. Mallory approached the end of her life, she did not want to see the land of her childhood developed in such a way. I believe she sold her land to me because she believed I loved the land as much as she did (exhibit 5-1).

CHAPTER 9

Trial by Jury Is Demanded

Mrs. Lorena Dobyns Conner died on January 25, 2011. Two months after she passed away I was asked by her son-in-law to show him the boundary between Parcels 20-90 and 20-91. I agreed to his request and we met for that purpose on April 9, 2011. I was surprised when his wife, Anita Conner Tadlock, and her uncle, Raymond E. Dobyns Jr., showed up as well. In 2011 I was still unaware that the boundary surveyed by Mr. C. E. Tomlin Jr. was inconsistent with the deeded description for that boundary. Consequently, I took the group down the Tomlin Line that I had maintained for thirty-six years. As we walked down that line, I mentioned my confusion about where Parcels 20-90, 20-91, and 20-131 came together. Neither Mr. C. E. Tomlin Jr. nor Mr. W. R. Keyser had shown that common point in their surveys. In fact, Mr. Keyser placed the label for Parcel 20-131 partially onto Parcel 20-90A, that Jena and I own (exhibit 6-7).

About two years after our walk Mrs. Tadlock and her uncle formed a limited liability corporation that they named Dobyns Family LLC. Mrs. Tadlock assumed management of that corporation when it began operation on January 10, 2013. Soon after beginning operation, Mrs. Tadlock hired Mr. Michael A. Wind to conduct a land survey of Dobyns Family LLC holdings. In his survey Mr. Wind followed the Tomlin Line for the boundary between Parcels 20-90 and 20-91 (exhibit 6-11). Mr. Wind indicated the land to the northwest of the Tomlin Line to be owned by Dobyns Family LLC. When I discovered this I was confused because in his survey of Parcel 20-90 on March 12, 1975, Mr. C. E. Tomlin Jr. indicated the land to the northwest of the line he drew to be owned by "*STONEHAM EST.*" Based on Mr. Tomlin's labeling I had understood for thirty-eight years that my land had a boundary with Parcel 20-131. Such boundary is described in the source deed for my land. It was puzzling to me that while Mr. Wind followed the Tomlin Line, his survey was not consistent with Mr. Tomlin's survey in that very significant way.

By late March 2013, Mr. Wind was approaching the end of his survey. On the evening of Thursday, March 28, 2013, as I was leaving my property, I observed a stake with blue ribbon tied to it placed on the *south* side of Jena's and my driveway. I knew Mr. Wind was using blue tape in his survey. But I was puzzled by the placement of that stake because I recognized immediately its placement was inconsistent with several previous surveys done for Jena and me by T&K, Inc. Because of the inconsistency, Jena and I were initially skeptical about the placement of Mr. Wind's stake. Still we knew this matter required investigation because the position of the stake clearly indicated our driveway was in question. The very next day, I began research. My research has now extended into six years. During those years I have learned truths that I never would have imagined.

In my early field work I used my old nautical sextant held horizontally for angular measurements and a three-hundred-foot reel tape for linear measurements. To my astonishment, after several days of hacking brush, stretching tape, and turning angles, I discovered that Mr. Wind's placement of the stake was correct. Two surveys by Tomlin and Keyser, Inc. were wrong about the southwest corner of Parcel 20-90 as *graphically* presented on their plats. I had not discovered the problem because I had not previously measured the 751.47 feet northward, through thicket and boggy area, to the black gum tree (exhibit 6-12, top photo). But during this early field work I discovered another error that perturbed me even more than the misplacement of the southwest corner. I discovered that neither Mr. C. E. Tomlin Jr. nor Mr. W. R. Keyser had turned a right angle at the southwest corner of Parcel 20-90. This meant the western boundary drawn by Mr. C. E. Tomlin Jr. that I had demonstrated to the Tadlocks and to Mr. R. E. Dobyns Jr. was wrong. The source deed for Parcel 20-90 clearly calls for a right angle at the southwest corner of my land. Disbelieving my initial angular measurement, I adjusted the index mirror on my sextant and repeated the measurement. When I got home, I calculated mathematically the angle derived from the identical entering and departing bearings at the southwest corner given on both Mr. Tomlin's and Mr. Keyser's plats. The calculated angle matched my sextant angle, and it was *not* a ninety degree angle! Here was proof that my T&K, Inc. surveys were not consistent with my deed. Two surveyors had not turned a right angle very clearly described in the deed for the land they were surveying.

From my early research I came to two conclusions. First, a fifteen foot wide strip of the driveway my family had used for thirty-nine years, and that we thought we owned by purchase from the Bartlett family, actually belonged to Dobyns Family LLC. Second, the western boundary certified by Mr. C. E. Tomlin Jr. on March 12, 1975, and thereafter followed by Mr. W. R. Keyser in his survey of May 28, 1997, was wrong.

Early in the summer of 2013, Dobyns Family LLC began logging operations. The contractor was Campbell Logging Company. Early in the logging, I spoke with Armando, the company's on-site foreman. Standing with him at the southwest corner of Parcel 20-90, I read the description in my deed. I had set out a 3:4:5 triangle with the right angle at the stake set by Mr. Wind. Armando and I then walked the Downing Line to the cedar stob that Mr. Wind had set on the boundary with Parcel 20-131. Following our meeting, Armando advised his boss of our conversation. When I next saw Armando, he informed me that he had been ordered not to cut in the disputed area.

About two weeks later, as I was leaving my property, I observed many young trees lying on the ground in the disputed area. The trees had been cut haphazardly at knee height. It was an impassable mess! When Armando saw me, he rushed to explain that his crew had nothing to do with the destruction. He told me about his discussion with the forestry consultant hired by Dobyns Family LLC. Armando said the consultant was upset when told that Campbell Logging Company would not cut in the disputed area. I reported the malicious act to the sheriff and to the state forester.

After Campbell Logging Company finished timber cutting, all was quiet on the western boundary until shortly before Thanksgiving, 2013. A few days before Thanksgiving, a deputy from the Lancaster County Sheriff's Office delivered two summonses at our house, one for Jena and one for me. Jena signed for both summonses because, as a member of the Lancaster County School Board, I was at the Virginia School Board Association conference in Williamsburg, Virginia on the day of delivery. During Thanksgiving dinner that year, as we sat with family and friends, Jena and I were under great emotional strain. We knew from the summonses that if we did not respond within twenty-one days, the allegations and charges against us might be taken as admitted and the court might enter an order, judgment, or decree against us. We knew that a judgment against us would impair our deed. Even though we knew that it would be a long and expensive ordeal, Jena and I felt compelled to proceed in defense of our deed. We sought help from the law firm Dunton, Simmons & Dunton, LLP. The attorney assigned to our case was Mr. Michael L. Donner Sr. Mr. Donner prepared the required "pleading in writing, in proper legal form," and Case Number CL13-83 was docketed in Lancaster Circuit Court. Of importance to the forthcoming civil trial was the fact that the plaintiff, Dobyns Family LLC, demanded trial by jury.

During much of 2014, Jena and I were involved in preparation for the trial. After listening to our problem, Mr. Donner exhibited a good understanding of the technical aspects of the case. To assist him,

Dunton, Simmons & Dunton, LLP recommended as expert witness Mr. Charles R. Pruett. I am especially thankful for that recommendation. Mr. Pruett has stood by my side even after the trial. Both Mr. Donner and Mr. Pruett felt that Jena and I had a strong case. The description for the disputed boundary, written by Mr. Thomas J. Downing in the source deed for our property and iterated in the source deed for the adjoining Dobyns Family LLC property, was clear. And no documentation could be found to support the line drawn by Mr. C. E. Tomlin Jr.

However, about a month before the trial Mr. Pruett prophetically warned Jena and me that jury trials can be unpredictable. He opined that although our case seemed solid, jurors are sometimes swayed by arguments that sound appealing but that lack foundation. Mr. Pruett was prescient. It is often said that we grow too soon old and too late wise. That certainly seems true for me in this case. I see now that if I had asked Mr. Pruett to survey *all* of Parcel 20-90 before the trial, things might have turned out differently. Mr. Pruett is a very experienced and conscientious surveyor, and I feel certain that a survey by him of Parcel 20-90 would have discovered the many faults in Mr. C. E. Tomlin's survey before the trial. With evidence of those faults the jury might not have been so quick to dismiss Mr. Downing's deeds in favor of an acreage apportionment argument. But Mr. Pruett was only asked to survey the disputed area, showing the Downing Line that Mr. Wind refused to show on his plat.

Prior to trial, the plaintiff attempted to estop a defense by Jena and me. I believe this effort was based on the fact that I had demonstrated the Tomlin Line to Mr. and Mrs. Tadlock and to Mr. Raymond E. Dobyns Jr. on April 9, 2011. But in a pre-trial hearing, the case was permitted to go forward. I believe the judge's decision was based on a 1921 Virginia Supreme Court case. In Bradshaw v. Booth, 129 Va. 19, 105 S. E. 555 [1921], the Virginia Supreme Court held:

"No mere parol agreement to establish a boundary and thus exclude from the operation of a deed land embraced therein can divest, change or effect the legal rights of the parties growing out of the deed itself."

The Bradshaw v. Booth Case involved a boundary dispute where a survey had been done many years before and had gone unchallenged. A lower court had ruled in favor of estoppel to block the defendant from later challenging the survey based on his lengthy acquiescence. The Virginia Supreme Court reversed the ruling of the lower court when it held:

"The instruction rests upon the position that the mere acquiescence of the defendant mentioned estopped him from afterwards asserting any adverse claim of title inconsistent with the validity of the survey in the accuracy of which he had acquiesced."

The Virginia Supreme Court went on to say:

"Mere acquiescence does not operate as an estoppel in such case, for the reason that, if this were so, such acquiescence would be given the effect of an independent source of title."

A few days before the trial, Dobyns Family LLC offered a settlement that involved moving the southwest corner of Parcel 20-90 eastward. This would have had the same effect as Mr. Warren Keyser's driveway survey of July 13, 1973, where he located the southwest cornerstone 35.4 feet farther east than his partner, Mr. C. E. Tomlin Jr., found it on March 12, 1975. The settlement offer seemed strange because the southwest corner had been recovered by the plaintiff's own expert witness, and Jena and I had agreed to that point. Mr. C. E. Tomlin Jr. had determined that point by measurements to three known marks, and the plaintiff's expert witness averred that he could find no fault in Mr. Tomlin's survey.

Mr. Raymond E. Dobyns Sr., Mr. Louis O. Cox, and Mrs. Rosa E. Thomas were each a party to petition for the agreement at the hearing on April 9, 1912. The three were all present several months later at the ceremony to bury the stone. By dint of these actions, those three are the highest authority as to placement of the stone. All three went to their graves with no expressed desire to move the stone. The position of the stone was agreed upon by the plaintiff and the defendant. Why then should the southwest corner be moved? After consultation with Mr. Donner, Jena and I decided not to accept the settlement offer to move the southwest corner. We then made a counteroffer as follows: 1) Dobyns Family LLC would agree to the line "A-F" as shown on the survey by Mr. Charles R. Pruett; 2) the Smarts would remove their encroaching driveway; and 3) each party would grant the other a mutual release of claims. Our counteroffer was rejected by the plaintiff. It became clear there would be a trial.

From the outset of the trial the plaintiff gave a well-presented argument for determining the disputed boundary based on acreage apportionment *under terms of the 1912 agreement.* Jena and I were not prepared to counter the acreage testimony presented by the plaintiff in support of this argument because we had not asked Mr. Pruett to survey all of Parcel 20-90. I cannot condemn the jury for accepting the acreage apportionment argument, nor for accepting the acreage testimony given in support of that argument. After all, it is true that the deeds arose out of the agreement. And after all, the acreage testimony for Parcel 20-90 was based on Mr. C. E. Tomlin's certified survey that I had recorded years before. Surveys had been done for all three parcels growing out of the Cox farm subdivision and it seems to have been tacitly accepted that all the acreage testimony given to the jury was apropos of the agreement. I believe that only a survey by Mr. Pruett demonstrating that the testimony given with regard to Parcel 20-90 was not correct, would have stood any chance of convincing the jury that a decision based on acreage testimony should not prevail over the deeds.

As mentioned, the plaintiff argued that the deeds must reflect the terms of the agreement out of which the deeds arose. The plaintiff argued that the deeds did not properly apportion the acreage in the Cox farm according to the agreement, and the agreement should prevail. As a consequence of the apparent acceptance of this reasoning by the jury, the deeds describing the boundary in dispute were rendered effectively inconsequential in determining the disputed boundary.

During the trial I was questioned on the witness stand about the acreage testimony that had been given for Parcels 20-90 and 20-91. I challenged the accuracy of that acreage testimony, but I do not believe my testimony was effective before the jury. Here is dialogue from the trial transcript, page 110, where the plaintiff's attorney questions me on acreage:

Q You regard the acreages of being of no particular significance in terms of the location of the property line?
A There was no acreage that could have been determined from my survey that says 25 acres. You can calculate the acreage of an "O" because it's a closed figure. You cannot calculate the acreage of a "C". It's not a closed figure. The Tomlin survey was not a closed figure.

Q My question was –
A Twenty-five acres means nothing. I did not take into account any acreage in the determination of Line AF – or the line that we now call AF.

Q And, in fact, you're not able – even sitting here today – to say what the resulting acreage would be to you or to Dobyns based upon that line AF; is that correct?
A That's true.

Q You just regard it as a nonfactor?

A Both the Dobyns property and my property have not had surveys that are closed.

Here is what Virginia Code 18VAC10-20-370, paragraph C.3 says about closing a boundary survey:

> *"For a land boundary survey located in a rural area, the maximum permissible error of closure for a field traverse shall be one part in 10,000 (1/10,000). The attendant angular closure shall be that which will sustain the one part in 10,000 (1/10,000) maximum error of closure."*

Mr. C. E. Tomlin Jr. did not measure along the waterfront of Senior Creek – a linear distance of over seven hundred feet – in his survey of Parcel 20-90 (exhibit 6-4). Thus, he did not close his survey. Still, he labeled his work, "A Boundary Survey of the Land of Robert V. Smart." It is difficult to imagine that an experienced certified land surveyor such as Mr. C. E. Tomlin Jr. did not know that he must survey the entire boundary of a tract in order to call it a boundary survey and to certify acreage.

Regarding Mr. M. A. Wind's failure to close a boundary survey before certifying acreage for Parcel 20-91, he did not give measurement along the western boundary of that parcel. That boundary is about one thousand nine hundred feet in length, and it is the boundary that separates Parcel 20-91 (the land purchased by Mr. R. E. Dobyns in 1912) from Parcel 20-98 (the original Dobyns family homestead). Mr. Wind wrote on his plat: *"Internal parcel. Line not surveyed at this time (typical) (See note: 3)."* In note 3 Mr. Wind wrote: *"The internal boundaries shown here were not surveyed at this time; however, it is the desire of the owner that these parcels remain separate and distinct"* (exhibit 6-11). If the owner of Parcels 20-91 and 20-98 wanted to keep those parcels "separate and distinct", why was the hedgerow along Mr. T. H. Warner's eastern survey line of Parcel 20-98 destroyed (exhibit 6-3)? Mr. Wind stated in testimony that he computed this line, but that does not meet the standards for closure of a survey in Virginia. Further, Mr. Wind did not monument that line. Here is what Virginia Code 18VAC10-20-370, paragraph C.4 says about the need to monument:

> *"As a requisite for completion of the work product, each land boundary survey of a tract or parcel of land shall be monumented with objects made of permanent material at all corners and changes of direction on the land boundary."*

Mr. Wind did not close and did not monument a boundary survey of Parcel 20-91. For that reason he should not have certified acreage for that parcel.

Nevertheless, Mr. Wind certified Parcel 20-91 to contain: "26 AC. +/- north of the road" and "17 ¾ AC. +/- south of the road" for a total of forty-three and three quarter acres, following the Tomlin Line (exhibit 6-11). This survey was entered as an exhibit early on in the trial. But later in the trial Mr. Wind gave oral testimony that must have caused the jury to reconsider the certified acreage in the survey exhibit. The following is that testimony, from page 131 of the trial transcript:

> *"Bob Smart would have 25 acres, according to the Tomlin & Keyser plat; and the Dobyns family, in this parcel here, would have 44 and a half. If you include the take from the highway department, they would have 44 and a half."*

It was correct for Mr. Wind to clarify that acreage had been taken by the state to create the public right-of-way for VSH 662. That road did not exist in 1912. A portion of the original conveyance by Mr. T. J. Downing to Mr. R. E. Dobyns was given up to create that road.

The eastern boundary of Mr. T. J. Downing's conveyance to Mr. R. E. Dobyns was based on the description written by Mr. Downing to Mrs. Thomas. Mr. Downing made that clear in his deed to Mr. Dobyns. It would be sixty-three more years before Mr. C. E. Tomlin Jr. invented a new boundary. But what the jury needed to reach an equitable decision, after choosing to follow an acreage apportionment argument, was a precise determination of the acreage conveyed to Mr. R. E. Dobyns by Mr. T. J. Downing on April 30, 1912. To reach that determination, the following would be required: first, a properly closed survey of Parcel 20-91 as it exists today following the Tomlin Line; second, to the above survey must be added the acreage, determined by survey, taken from the original conveyance to create the current forty-foot wide public right of way for VSH 662; and finally, from this total must be subtracted 1.842 acres to account for the fact that Mr. Downing's conveyance to Mr. R. E. Dobyns was based on the Downing Line. Unfortunately the jury did not have such a precise determination. It was left guessing. Nor did the jury have accurate information for the acreage of Parcel 20-90, although it was unaware of this fact.

Given the terms of the agreement and the wording of the 1912 court decree, it is possible to analyze what Mr. Downing was instructed to do. When this analysis is done, the mathematics works out perfectly. The agreement states that there were eighty-six acres in the Cox farm (exhibit 1-2). Mr. Downing was ordered by the court to first convey to Mr. Louis O. Cox the *twenty and three quarter acres* surveyed by Mr. Herbert P. Hall. That left sixty-five and a quarter acres to divide between Mr. Raymond E. Dobyns and Mrs. Rosa E. Thomas. The agreement called for Mr. Dobyns to get two-thirds of those sixty-five and a quarter acres, or *forty-three and a half acres*. The agreement called for Mrs. Thomas to get one-third of the sixty-five and a quarter acres, or *twenty-one and three quarter acres*. Mr. Downing was instructed by the court to submit his work to the court at its next session. Surely he would not have knowingly disobeyed the court's instructions per the agreement it had approved. But Mr. Downing did not have an electronic calculator in 1912 and he might have been in a hurry to write the deeds. Perhaps he erred in his calculations. I believe Mr. T. J. Downing meant to convey twenty-one and three quarter acres to Mrs. Thomas and not twenty-three and three quarter acres. Presuming that Mr. Downing intended to follow the agreement and the instructions of the court, he would have conveyed twenty and three quarter acres to Mr. Cox; next he would have conveyed twenty-one and three quarter acres to Mrs. Thomas; and finally he would have conveyed forty-three and a half acres to Mr. Dobyns. By doing so, the acreage in the three parcels created from the subdivision of the Cox farm would total eighty-six acres.

The following acreages were given in trial testimony for the three parcels created from the Cox farm. For Parcel 20-89, twenty and three quarter acres (from Mr. Hall's closed survey). For Parcel 20-90, twenty-five acres (from Mr. Tomlin's unclosed survey). And for Parcel 20-91, forty-three and three quarter acres (from Mr. Wind's unclosed survey). But an amendment to the acreage for Parcel 20-91 was given as forty-four and one half acres (by Mr. Wind's oral testimony). The total acreages given in testimony all exceed the eighty-six acres subject to the agreement. From this an excellent question arises. *Where did the extra acreage come from?*

Jury instructions were to choose either the Downing or the Tomlin Line. Compromise was not permitted. If the jury chose not to follow the deeds but to determine the disputed boundary based on acreage apportionment, as it evidently did, it was forced to deliberate on the basis of the acreage testimony it heard. The jury had no idea that the testimony it heard for Parcel 20-90 was grossly inaccurate. *Four acres not subject to the subdivision agreement for the Cox farm had been added to Parcel 20-90.* The addition of those four acres renders the plaintiff's argument non sequitur. The plaintiff argued that terms of the agreement regarding the division of acreage should take precedence over the deeds written to execute the agreement. But terms of the agreement were then violated by the addition of acreage outside the agreement.

I believe that Mr. M. A. Wind was aware that acreage is the lowest factor to be considered in boundary determination. The following dialogue is from page 31 of a deposition given by Mr. Wind to Mr. Michael L. Donner Sr. three weeks before the trial:

> *Q Is there in the surveying business, is there a hierarchy of importance in what you look at as far as setting a boundary?*
> *A Yes.*
>
> *Q And what is your understanding of that hierarchy of importance?*
> *A You're asking me a question and putting me on the spot now.*
>
> *Q Take your time. I'm not trying to put you on the spot.*
> *A There are generally five things; there are natural boundaries, manmade boundaries, distances, bearings, and then acreage.*
>
> *Q Okay. Did you just list them in the order of priority?*
> *A Yes.*
>
> *Q Okay. So I noticed that you listed acreage last, correct?*
> *A Yes.*
>
> *Q So if there were - obviously a source deed or a source document would have to be the first priority. Would that be a true statement?*
> *A Yes.*
>
> *Q Okay. So if a source deed conflicts with an acreage measurement, the source deed would take priority over the acreage measurement in that hierarchy you just gave me; is that correct?*
> *A Yes.*

It is clear Mr. Wind understood that a deed stands higher in the hierarchy for boundary determination than acreage. Yet during the trial Mr. Wind argued for acreage over deed. Here is a bit of dialogue between Mr. Donner and Mr. Wind from page 91 of the trial transcript that demonstrates this:

> **Q** *So if it's reasonable to disagree with the line that you have shown on Plaintiff's Exhibit 3, it follows, doesn't it, that it's reasonable to show that – or to understand, or to find that Mr. Smart's line is correct?*
> **A** *No, because the problem with Mr. Smart's line is not that it's straight, not that it doesn't turn a 90-degree angle. The problem with Mr. Smart's line is it doesn't distribute the acreage.*
>
> **Q** *So, we're again back to the acreage?*
> **A** *Exactly. That's the problem with Mr. Smart's property, is the acreage.*

As the jury began deliberations, it first had to decide what acreage it would use for Parcel 20-91. Should the jury use the forty-three and three quarter acres certified by Mr. Wind in his survey where he followed the Tomlin Line and excluded the acreage originally conveyed to Mr. R. E. Dobyns but now taken up in VSH 662? Or should the jury use the forty-four and one half acres following the Tomlin Line that Mr. Wind gave in oral testimony? The jury probably did not consider the fact that Mr. Wind's survey was not properly closed.

The jury probably had no reservations at all about the acreage testimony for Parcel 20-90. After all, Mr. C. E. Tomlin Jr. had certified Parcel 20-90 to be 25.0 acres on March 12, 1975 and his partner, Mr. W. R. Keyser, had certified Parcel 20-90 to be 24.96 acres on May 28, 1997. I had recorded both those surveys years before, and Mr. Wind had stated that he could find no fault with Mr. Tomlin's survey. Again, the fact that Mr. Tomlin's survey was not properly closed was probably not considered.

It must have seemed clear to the jury that Parcel 20-90 contained *three and a quarter acres more* than the twenty-one and three quarter acres it should receive as its one-third share under the agreement, while Parcel 20-91 contained about *one acre more* than the forty-three and one half acres it should receive as its two-thirds share under the agreement. On that basis the jury's selection of the Tomlin Line appears to be the correct choice. Certainly the *logic* of the jury's decision *based on the testimony it heard* is correct, and the jury did not know the information it heard was not correct. The jury had been led astray by an appealing but poorly founded argument. Mr. Pruett's concerns had become reality.

The total acreage being considered by the jury was ninety and one quarter acres, as twenty and three quarter acres for Parcel 20-89; twenty-five acres for Parcel 20-90; and forty-four and one half acres for Parcel 20-91. This is more than four acres greater than the area of the Cox farm. How might the jury have reasoned if it had known where the extra four acres came from? The jury very likely would have corrected downward the area of Parcel 20-90 from twenty-five acres to twenty-one acres following the Tomlin Line. This is *three quarter acre less* than Parcel 20-90 is due under the agreement. Similarly, the jury very likely would have observed that Parcel 20-91 remained forty-four and one half acres following the Tomlin Line, per Mr. Wind's oral testimony. This is *one acre more* than Parcel 20-91 is due under the agreement. At that point one juror might have stated: *"I feel more comfortable now that we have learned of the error in acreage because now I see the total acreage being considered is very close to the eighty-six acres described in the agreement."*

But then another juror, who might have remained quiet up to this time, might have broken her silence. With clarity and excellent rationale she might have gone straight to the heart of the matter by saying:

> **"The plaintiff desires to determine a boundary within a land subdivision that is based on acreage apportionment under terms of a court approved agreement. The agreement is specific as to acreage**

apportionment and as to the acreage of the land being subdivided. The acreage testimony we have heard to support the plaintiff's argument is not apropos of the agreement because the acreage testimony we have heard exceeds the acreage stated in the agreement. The addition of four acres outside the agreement exposes a serious flaw in the plaintiff's argument. Those additional acres were never part of the land being subdivided and are thus not subject to the subdivision agreement. As a result, the plaintiff's argument does not logically follow and we as the jury cannot reach an equitable determination of boundary based on acreage information we have been given.

Further, it appears that other acreage testimony we were given may be flawed. For example, we were given acreage testimony derived from two land surveys that were not closed according to state surveying regulations. Those surveys are of the parcels lying on either side of the boundary in question. As well, acreage was taken on two occasions from the original conveyance for one parcel in order to create a public right-of-way and we do not know the precise amount of the taking.

We have been asked to determine which one of two lines is the true boundary between Parcels 20-90 and 20-91. The description for the first of the two lines is contained in the source deeds for both of those parcels. Those deeds were written by Mr. Downing, who was appointed a special commissioner by the court that approved the agreement. The deeds he wrote were then promulgated by that court. The description for the boundary now in dispute is clear in the source deeds for both tracts lying on either side of the boundary in dispute. Both those deeds were recorded and remained unchallenged during the lifetimes of all parties to the agreement. The deeds written by Mr. Downing are legal authority to convey real estate.

The second of the two lines was created sixty-three years after the deeds were written, as part of a survey that we now know is faulty because it is inconsistent with several deeds on record at the time the survey was done. There is no documentation to support the survey. Surveys per se are not legal authority to convey real estate.

In my opinion the acreage apportionment argument we have heard is not well founded. I believe it would be wrongheaded for us to overturn a documented line to select an undocumented line based on acreage testimony that is known to be erroneous. Based on what we now know it appears that selecting the undocumented survey line would give Parcel 20-91 more than it is due under the agreement and would give Parcel 20-90 less than it is due under the agreement.

I believe that the work done by Mr. Hall, by the 1912 court, and by Mr. Downing to subdivide the Cox farm was accomplished with care and understanding. I do not believe the 1975 survey of Parcel 20-90 was done with care.

I believe we should honor the 1912 deeds by selecting the Downing Line as the true boundary."

Perhaps after a moment of collective reflection the jury *might* then have upheld the work of Lancaster Circuit Court from April 1912. Unfortunately the jury never came to know about Ada's land.

I believe the survey work of Mr. Charles E. Tomlin Jr. in the subject area has created a chaos of confusion. I believe that among those ensnared in this confusion were the judge and jurors in Lancaster Circuit Court on September 11, 2014.

I have a Veteran's Administration (VA) rating for bi-lateral hearing loss incurred during my service in USS *Galveston* (CLG-3). I was wearing my VA-issued hearing aids on the day of the trial, yet I still could not hear the proceedings. During an early break in the trial, I informed the Clerk of the Circuit Court of my inability to hear the proceedings. She informed me the sound system was broken and could not be fixed that day. After the trial the Clerk wrote a letter to provide documentation of my request to turn up the sound system (exhibit 9-2). Before receiving that letter I filed a complaint with the Virginia Judicial System, Americans with Disabilities Act (ADA) Compliance Officer. Within a few days, the Compliance Officer called to advise me that action had been taken to fix the sound system. But the fact remains that I, the defendant, could not hear the trial proceedings and accommodation could not be made.

The decree stemming from the trial in Lancaster Circuit Court on September 11, 2014 nullified a boundary described in two deeds promulgated by Lancaster Circuit Court one hundred and two years before.

The decree divests the legal rights of parties growing out of a lawful deed.

The decree establishes a new source of title based on a land survey that is known to be inconsistent with multiple deeds recorded prior to the survey.

The decree may be inconsistent with a previous higher court ruling.

The defendant could not hear the proceedings of the trial due to a stated hearing disability.

CHAPTER 10

Epilogue

The Department of Professional and Occupational Regulation (DPOR) has oversight responsibility for the conduct of land surveying in Virginia. To accomplish this responsibility DPOR issues licenses to certify land surveyors. DPOR also publishes surveying standards for certified land surveyors to follow. Finally, DPOR investigates complaints against land surveyors.

Jena and I believe the DPOR certification program is good. We also believe the Minimum Standards and Procedures for Land Boundary Surveying Practice in Virginia (18VAC10-20-370) are well written. But we believe the integrity of land surveying in Virginia is diminished because DPOR is not properly enforcing its standards and procedures. Jena and I have experienced that the receipt of a certified survey in Virginia is no guarantee the work is compliant with DPOR standards or is true to deeds on record at the time of the survey.

Jena and I believe the great majority of certified land surveyors in Virginia perform their work with faithfulness, understanding and care, adhering to published standards and to documentation on record. But we believe, based on personal experience, this is not true in every case. The government often requires surveys to be conducted in order to get building permits or to proceed with land utilization. Given this requirement, Jena and I believe the government bears a responsibility to ensure surveys are conducted with care. Certified surveys should not cause unwarranted harm to land owners. Jena and I believe we have paid for required surveys that have caused us unwarranted harm.

The foregoing work is not so much intended as an indictment of any surveyor's methods or misapplication of professional guidelines, as it is a cautionary tale about blindly trusting the measurements given in a previous survey rather than conducting the scrupulous research of land records required to discover the truth contained in recorded deeds. It is also a cautionary tale that disputes of land boundaries, which often involve technical survey standards, are best not resolved by lay jurors unfamiliar with the standards and technology behind land surveying.

Following the trial on September 11, 2014 I made known to DPOR my concerns that the integrity of land surveying in Virginia was being compromised because of weak enforcement of published DPOR survey standards and procedures. Two years of correspondence with DPOR followed. After such lengthy correspondence I concluded that I would not be able to educe what I believe to be needed reform by appeal through bureaucracy. I had apparently come up against a bureaucratic wall. As I still believe that reform is needed, I sought a different course. I abandoned my effort at reform through DPOR in order to write this book.

I sincerely hope my redirected effort will bear fruit by helping others to avoid situations similar to what Jena and I have endured, and possibly by ultimately securing needed reform at DPOR. If the Virginia DPOR fails in its mission to ensure integrity of land surveying, great harm is done both to individuals and to the economy at large. I believe Jena's and my experience shows that *reforms are needed*. I believe it is time for the Governing Board for Architects, Professional Engineers, Land

Surveyors, Certified Interior Designers and Landscape Architects (APELSCIDLA Board) to conduct a *comprehensive restructuring* of land surveying enforcement procedures at the Department of Professional and Occupational Regulation. It seems clear that if a citizen is required by government to obtain a land survey and the citizen complies with the requirement by contracting a state certified land surveyor, then the government bears some responsibility to ensure that the certified survey does not harm the citizen's lawful estate.

Land surveying is vital to the economy of Virginia. The surveying profession requires both technical knowledge and integrity. In 1705 the Virginia Legislature wrote: *"The quiet of our estates, in a great measure, depends upon the faithfulness, understanding, and care of our surveyors."* That is as true now as it was then. Over a period of twenty-six years, from 1971 to 1997, the Smart family paid for four certified land surveys. At the time each of those surveys was received, we believed them to have been accomplished with care. I believe it was not unreasonable to have such confidence. However, I now believe those surveys were not conducted with care, and Jena and I have suffered as a result. We have lost land; we have lost money; and we have suffered prolonged emotional distress.

Most people do not have the technical knowledge to verify surveys on their own. They should not be required to do so. It should be presumable that a certified survey complies with state surveying standards and is true to deeds on record at the time of the survey.

In closing, I advise every land owner to carefully read their deed and to fully understand it. Also, carefully review any surveys done of your land. Are your surveys consistent with your deeds? Compare your surveys to surveys done of adjoining lands. Are your surveys consistent with those of adjoining lands? Compare your deed to the deeds for adjoining lands. Is there any conflicting language or inconsistency? If you don't feel knowledgeable enough to do this, you should have an attorney review pertinent documentation. Any inconsistencies discovered should be dealt with right away. The best answer for most boundary issues is to carefully "read the deed", understand it on the ground, and make sure that once understanding is reached the correct boundary is monumented and honored. The boundary should be inspected on the ground every few years. Don't prolong poorly understood boundaries; get them clarified.

Jena and I were greatly assisted in writing this book by Mr. Charles R. Pruett. We were also assisted by my brother, Colonel Neil A. Smart, who is retired from the U. S. Army Corps of Engineers, with specialty in highway engineering. Mrs. Diane Mumford, the Clerk of Lancaster Circuit Court, and her staff were very helpful. Following the trial, Mrs. Mumford obtained for me copies of the 1912 agreement and the resulting 1912 Lancaster Circuit Court proceedings from the Library of Virginia. Also, her staff was very patient to teach me how to conduct research in the Records Room.

Lancaster County, Virginia, has some of the oldest land records in the United States and those records are very well kept. This book would not have been possible without the meticulous work of past Clerks of Lancaster Circuit Court. The following Clerks filed records that were used to write this book: Mr. Oscar Chilton, Mr. William Chilton, Mr. Warner Eubank, Mrs. Roberta Lewis, Mrs. Constance Oliver, and Mrs. Diane Mumford.

May peace be with all.

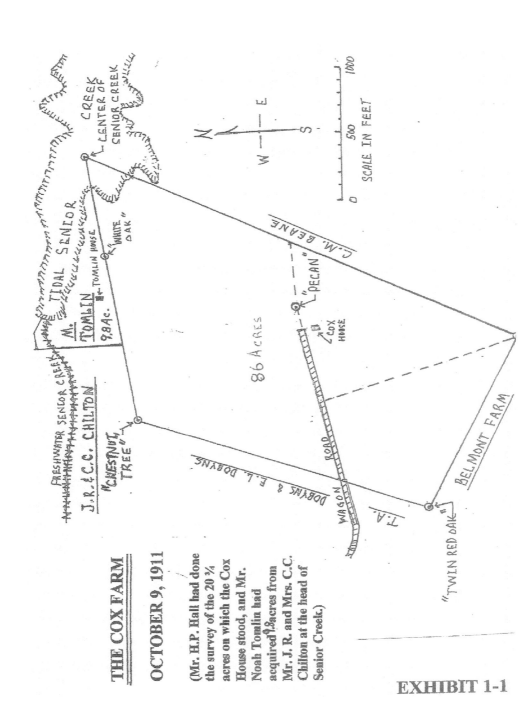

THE COX FARM

OCTOBER 9, 1911

(Mr. H.P. Hall had done the survey of the 20 ¾ acres on which the Cox House stood, and Mr. Noah Tomlin had acquired 9.8 acres from Mr. J. R. and Mrs. C.C. Chilton at the head of Senior Creek.)

CREEK
CENTER OF SENIOR CREEK

N
W — E
S
SCALE IN FEET
0   500   1000

FRESHWATER SENIOR CREEK

M. TIDAL SENIOR

"WHITE OAK"

TOMLIN HOUSE

TOMLIN
9.8 AC.

J.R. & C.C. CHILTON

"CHESTNUT TREE"

C.M. BEANE

"PECAN"

COX HOUSE

86 ACRES

DOBYNS & F.L. DOBYNS

WAGON ROAD

T.A.

BELMONT FARM

"TWIN RED OAK"

EXHIBIT 1-1

– 102 –

THE AGREEMENT

.

R. E. Dobyns et als

vs.

Filed: April 9, 1912
Teste. Wm. Chilton, Clerk

E. L. Haynie et als

To the Hon. T. R. B. Wright, Judge of the Circuit Court of Lancaster County, Va.

Your Complainants Lewis O. Cox, R. E. Dobyns, Rosa E. Thomas, who was Rosa E. Cox, and E. L. Thomas her husband, humbly complaining showeth unto the Court that Elnora B. Cox who was the wife of the said Lewis O. Cox, but who is now dead, acquired by devise from Nancy Biscoe a certain tract or parcel of land lying in White Chapel district Lancaster County Va. That later to wit on the 15th day of May 1882, the said Elnora B. Cox purchased of Warner W. Beane and Mary A. Beane, his wife, another tract or parcel of land lying contiguous to the land so devised to her the said Elnora B. Cox by Nancy Biscoe. That the two tracts of land thus lying together comprise eighty six acres and have been used as one farm – and occupied as a home by the said Lewis O. Cox and his wife Elnora B. Cox during the life time of the said Elnora B. Cox and since her death, which occurred about the year by the said Lewis O. Cox, who has remained in possession of same as Tenant by the Curtesy.

The said Elnora B. Cox left surviving her the following Children viz. Mamie Cox, Rosa E. Cox, and Fannie Drew Cox: that the said Mamie Cox married one E.F. Haynie, and died about the year, leaving surviving her the following children - Lewis Franklin aged 13 years, Elnora L. aged nine years, McClinock aged seven years, Nellie aged five years, her only heirs at law and her husband the said E. F. Haynie - : That the said Rosa E. Cox married E. L. Thomas, and the said Fannie Drew Cox married one William Streets.

EXHIBIT 1-2

Your Complainants beg leave to further show unto the Court that on the 15th day of May 1882 the said Lewis O. Cox and Elnora B. Cox his wife borrowed from the Trustees of the Glebe Fund of Lancaster County the sum of Three hundred and forty one dollars and eighty four cents ($341.84) and on the same date executed a deed of trust on the said eighty six acres of land hereinbefore mentioned, to secure the said debt - which said deed of trust is herewith filed marked Exhibit "A" and asked to be read as a part of the bill. Your complainants show unto the Court that no part of the principal of said debt has been paid and that the interest on same is in arrears for several years – leaving still and on interest the sum of $89.00.

That the said Fannie Drew Streets and her husband William Streets have sold their undivided interest in the said land subject to the said deed of trust and also to the life estate of the said Lewis O. Cox to R. E. Dobyns, one of your Complainants, for the sum of one hundred dollars as is shown by a deed from the said William Streets and wife to said R. E. Dobyns which is herewith shown unto the Court.

Your Complainants further show unto the Court that the said E. F. Haynie can effect a sale of the interest in the land owned by his infant children as aforesaid as well as his life estate in said interest as Tenant by the Curtesy to the said R. E. Dobyns for the sum of Two hundred dollars, which said debt is to be payable in one year from date and the payment of same secured by deed of trust on the interest so acquired as well as on the interest acquired from the said Fannie Drew Streets. And your Complainants are advised and so state that the said E. F. Haynie is anxious to effect said sale if the honorable Court will so decree. That an agreement has been reached between the said R. E. Dobyns, Rosa E. Thomas, E. L. Thomas and Lewis O. Cox that in case the Court sanctions the proposal of sale herein stated that the said R. E. Dobyns who will in that event be the holder of a two thirds undivided interest and the said Rosa E. Thomas who is the holder of a one third undivided interest, both interests however subject to the lien of the deed of trust aforesaid as well the life estate of said Lewis O. Cox in said whole tract of land, will assure and pay or otherwise satisfy the principal part of the deed held by the said Trustees of the Glebe Fund of Lancaster Co. and further that the said Lewis O. Cox shall have a deed in fee simple for twenty and three quarters acres as same has been surveyed - see plat herewith filed – free from the encumbrance of the said deed of trust. And the said Lewis O. Cox on his part obligates to pay in full all interest due on the said debt held by the said Trustees of the Glebe Fund of Lancaster Co.

EXHIBIT 1-2

and to give up and relinquish his right as Tenant by the Curtesy in the said remainder of the said land and to pay all costs attending this litigation.

For as much therefore as the Complainants are remediless in the premises save by the aid of a Court of equity, they pray that the said E. F. Haynie, Lewis Franklin Haynie, Elnora L. Haynie, McClinock Haynie and Nellie Haynie may be made parties defendant to this bill and be required to answer. The same answers on oath being hereby specially waived that proper process issue, that this honorable Court by its decretal order sanction and confirm the bargain and agreement hereinbefore set out, and may also direct a sale of the interest in the said land to which the said infants are entitled in accordance with the proposal as above set out. That a Commissioner may be appointed to make to the proper parties deeds in accordance with said agreement. That all proper orders may be issued, inquiries directed and accounts taken as shall be necessary to arrive at a proper understanding of the rights and interests of the parties to these proceedings, and that all such other further, and general relief may be afforded your Complainants as is in accordance with equity and good conscience and your Complainants will as in duty bound ever pray so.

T. J. Downing

EXHIBIT 1-2

CONSENT DECREE TO THE AGREEMENT

Tuesday, April 9th 1912

Present,

Same judge as on March 22nd 1912.

R. E. Dobyns et als   }
vs   }
E. F. Haynie et als   }

This day came the Complainants by Counsel and by leave of the Court filed their bill, and the exhibits therewith. And on their motion P. M. Gresham a discreet and competent attorney at law is assigned as the guardian ad litum of the infants, Lewis Franklin Haynie, Elnora Haynie, McClinnock Haynie and Nellie Haynie, to defend their interests in this suit. And thereupon the said guardian ad litum filed this answer of the said infant defendants, and his own answer to the bill of complaint, and E. F. Haynie, the adult defendant filed his answer to the said bill, to which several answers the complainants replied generally. And thereupon by consent of all parties, by counsel, this cause is set for hearing, and docketed, and by like consent came on this day to be heard on the bill of complaint and the exhibits therewith, the several answers of the defendants to the said bill as above set out, and the general replication of complainants to every one of said answers, and was argued by Counsel. On consideration whereof the court doth adjudge, order and decree that this cause be referred to one of the Commissioners of this Court, who is directed to inquire and report to the Court as follows: 1st Of what real estate or interest in real estate the said infants are possessed of or entitled to, and what are their respective shares or interests therein, where such estate is situated, and what is its fee simple and annual value. 2nd Whether the interest of said infant defendants will be promoted by a sale of the real estate in the bill mentioned and on investment of the proceeds. 3rd Whether the rights of any person will be violated by such sale and investment. 4th Who would be the heirs at law or distributees of said infant defendants if they were dead, and whether all such persons are properly before the Court in this Cause. And the said Commissioner is directed if possible to make said inquiries and report to this Court at its present sitting.

EXHIBIT 1-3

R. E. Dobyns et als }
     vs   }
E. F. Haynie et als }

This cause came on again this day to be heard upon the papers formerly read and the report of R. O. Norris Jr., one of the Commissioners in Chancery of this Court, which said report was made and filed under a previous decree entered in this cause. And there being no exceptions to said report the same is hereby confirmed, and it appearing to the Court that the interests of the infant defendants will be promoted, and the interest of no person will suffer by a sale of the interest which the said infant children have in the land in the bill and proceedings mentioned, and the re-investment of the proceeds of sale. And it further appearing to the Court that R. E. Dobyns has purchased the interest of Fannie D. Streets in the said land and is now willing to purchase the interests of the said infants at the sum of two hundred dollars, and to secure the purchase price of said interest by bond or note, and deed of trust on the land so acquired from the said infants, as well as the land acquired from said Fannie D. Streets and husband, And it further appearing to the Court that the said R. E. Dobyns and L. O. Cox and Rosa E. Thomas, and E. L. Thomas, her husband, have agreed between themselves as to the division of the land above mentioned between themselves, and that according to said agreement the said L. O. Cox, who is tenant by the curtesy in the whole land is willing to pay the costs of these proceedings, as well as all interest in arrears on the debt due the Trustees of the Glebe Fund, and to give up and relinquish his right as tenant by curtesy in the whole land, provided he is given a fee simple estate in 20 ¾ acres of said land as same has been agreed upon and surveyed. And it still further appearing to the Court that the said R. E. Dobyns and said Rosa E. Thomas and E. L. Thomas, her husband, have agreed between themselves as to what portion of the remainder of said land they shall have, and the same having been argued by counsel, on consideration whereof the Court doth adjudge, order and decree that T. J. Downing, who is hereby appointed Special Commissioner for that purpose, is hereby directed to make and execute to the said L. O. Cox, or to such other person as he shall designate, a good and sufficient deed with special warranty of title to the twenty and three quarters acres of land in the bill mentioned, and in accordance with the survey recently made, - plat of which said survey has been shown to the Court – that the Commissioner aforesaid shall make to the said R. E. Dobyns a good and sufficient deed to

EXHIBIT 1-3

that portion of the remainder of said land which under the aforesaid agreement he is to have. And the said R. E. Dobyns shall make and execute a certain bond or note for $200 – Two hundred dollars payable to E. H. Haynie, Guardian for the said infants defendants, bearing interest from its date, and payable one year after date, and shall further execute a deed of trust on the land acquired as aforesaid by him to secure the payment of the said debt. And the said T. J. Downing, Commissioner as aforesaid shall execute a deed with special warranty of title to Rosa E. Thomas, or to such other person as she shall direct, for that part of said land she acquires under the said agreement above mentioned. And the said T. J. Downing, Special Commissioner as aforesaid, is directed to report his proceedings under the decree to the next term of this Court.

Ordered that this Court adjourn until the first day of next term.

J. R. B. Wright

R. E. Dobyns et als }
      vs   } Decree Entered, April 9, 1912
E. F. Haynie et als }   Hon. T. R. B. Wright , Judge of the Circuit Court
                                        Lancaster County, Va.

EXHIBIT 1-3

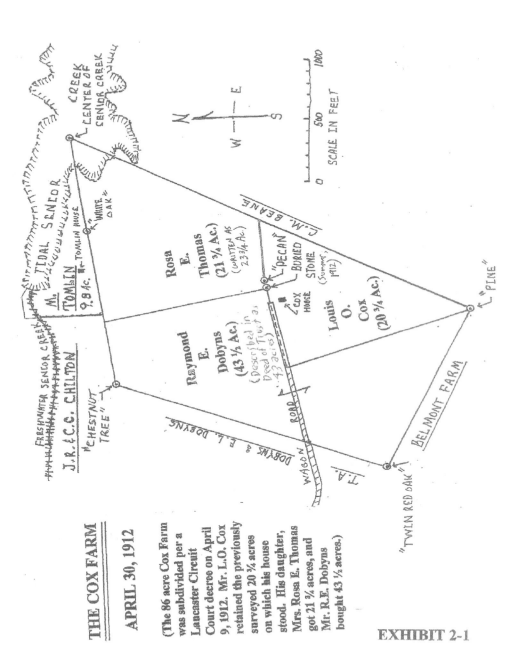

THE COX FARM

APRIL 30, 1912

(The 86 acre Cox Farm was subdivided per a Lancaster Circuit Court decree on April 9, 1912. Mr. L.O. Cox retained the previously surveyed 20 ¾ acres on which his house stood. His daughter, Mrs. Rosa E. Thomas got 21 ¾ acres, and Mr. R.E. Dobyns bought 43 ½ acres.)

EXHIBIT 2-1

CREEK
CENTER OF
SENIOR CREEK

N

W — E

S

0   500   1000
SCALE IN FEET

FRESHWATER SENIOR CREEK

TIDAL SENIOR

M. TOMLIN
9.8 AC. — TOMLIN HOUSE

"WHITE OAK"

J.R. & C.C. CHILTON

"CHESTNUT TREE"

Rosa E. Thomas
(21 ¾ Ac.)
(WRITTEN AS 23¾ Ac.)

C.J.M. BEANE

"PECAN"
BURIED STONE
(SUMMER, 1912)

Raymond E. Dobyns
(43 ½ Ac.)
(DESCRIBED IN DEED OF TRUST AS 43 ACRES)

COX HOUSE

Louis O. Cox
(20 ¾ Ac.)

"PINE"

WAGON ROAD

DOBYNS & E.L. DOBYNS

BELMONT FARM

"F.A."

"TWIN RED OAK"

This deed made and entered into this 30th day of April in the year 1916, by and between T. J. Downing who was appointed a Special Commissioner for that purpose party of the first part, and L. O. Cox party of the second part. Witnesseth that whereas by a decree pronounced in the Circuit Court of Lancaster County Va. in the Chancery cause therein depending under the style of R. E. Dobyns vs E. F. Haynie, the said T. J. Downing was appointed a Special Commissioner to execute certain deeds, amongst which was a one to said L. O. Cox, and whereas the conditions stipulated in the said decree with which the said L. O. Cox was to comply have been met, and now in consideration of the premises and by authority vested in the said T. J. Downing by the decree aforesaid, to which said decree reference is hereby made, Now this deed witnesseth that for the consideration aforesaid, the said T. J. Downing party of the first part has this day bargained and sold and by these presents does hereby bargain, sell, grant and convey unto the said L. O. Cox all of that certain tract or parcel of land lying in White Chapel Magisterial district in Lancaster County Va. which contains twenty and three quarters of an acre by actual survey, plat of which is herewith made a part of this deed and to be recorded herewith. Said land is bounded on the North by the lands of R. L. Beane and C. L. Beane. On the East by farm known as "Belle Mint". On the South by the lands this day conveyed by the said T. J. Downing to R. E. Dobyns. and on the West by the said land conveyed to said R. E. Dobyns and the land conveyed to Rosa E. —

To have and to hold the above described tract or parcel of land the said L. O. Cox and his heirs and assigns forever with special warranty of title. In testimony whereof witness the following hand and seal.

           T. J. Downing, Special Commissioner   (Seal)

Virginia:

In the Clerk's Office of the Circuit Court of Lancaster County, the 18th day of May, 1912, personally appeared T. J. Downing, whose name is signed to the within writing, bearing date on the 30th day of April, 1912, and acknowledged the same before me in the Clerk's Office aforesaid, whereupon said writing was admitted to record at 1.00 o'clock P.M.

         Teste:

              Wm. Chilton, Clerk

Margin notes (left): owning; Beane; of R.L.; Cox; Apr. 30-1912; May 18-1912; 20¾; not stated; Chapel; Per 1.25 .50; Acre 1.00 .50; + 22¾; to L.O.; Cox; Sept 9-1912 also

21.00 chains

N.

EXHIBIT 2-2

– 110 –

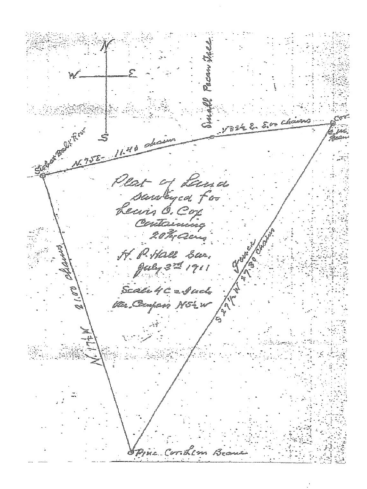

EXHIBIT 2-2
p. 2

– 111 –

This Deed made and entered into this 30th day of April 1912 and between T. G. Denning party of the first part and Rosa E. Thomas party of the second part witnesseth: that whereas, by certain decree pronounced by the Circuit Court of Lancaster Co. Va. on the 9th day of April 1912 in the Chancery cause therein depending under the name and style of R. E. Dobyns et al. vs. E. F. Haynie et als. the said T. G. Denning party of the first part was appointed a special Commissioner to execute said deed as therein provided for, and the conditions in the said deed provided for having been met, and the parties interested as heirs of the land of which Fluvia Cox died seized and possessed, having agreed amongst themselves as to a division of the said land, and now in order to give proper effect to the said decree this deed further witnesseth that for and in consideration of the premises and of other valuable consideration moving from the said Rosa E. Thomas party of the second part, the said T. G. Denning special commissioner as aforesaid has this day bargained and sold and by these presents does hereby bargain sell release and convey with special warranty of title, to the said Rosa E. Thomas all of their certain tract or parcel of land lying and being in White Chapel Magisterial district of Lancaster County Va. and said to contain 23¾ acres and which is further bounded and described as follows: to wit: On the North by the lands of Weldon Tomlin and lands of Mrs. C. C. Chilton On the East by Senior Creek the lands of C. W. Beane and on the South by the lands this day conveyed to L. O. Cox and on the west by the lands this day conveyed to R. E. Dobyns by T. G. Denning special commissioner the westward boundary is yet to be established by a survey of the land hereby conveyed which said westward boundary is to run at right angles to the line of the land of the said L. O. Cox as same has heretofore been surveyed And for that purpose reference is hereby made to the plat of said Coxes land made by H. P. Hall dated July 3 1911 and of record with the deed of said L. O. Cox — To have and to hold the said twenty three and three quarter acres of land with their appurtenances to her the said Rosa E. Thomas and her heirs and assigns forever — In testimony whereof Witness the following signature and seal

T. G. Denning (Seal)
Special Commissioner

EXHIBIT 2-3

Magisterial district of Lancaster County Va. and said to contain 28¾ acres and which is further bounded and described as follows-to-wit: On the North by the lands of Mollie Tomlin and lands of Mrs. C. C. Chilton. On the East by Senion Creek The lands of C. W. Beam and on the south by the lands this day conveyed to L. O. Cox and on the west by the lands this day conveyed to R. E. Dobyns by T. J. Downing Special Commissioner the westward boundary is yet to be established by a survey of the land hereby conveyed which said westward boundary is to run at right angles to the line of the land of the said R. O. Cox as same has heretofore been surveyed and for that purpose reference is hereby made to the plat of said Cox's land made by H. P. Hall dated July 3 1911 now of record with the deed of said L. O. Cox — To have and to hold the said twenty three and three quarter acres of land with their appurtenances to her the said Rosa E. Thomas and her heirs and assigns forever — In testimony whereof Witness the following signature and seal _____

                 T. J. Downing [seal]
                 Special Commissioner

Virginia, Lancaster County, To wit:
I, R. O. Norris, Jr. a Commissioner in Chancery of the Circuit Court of Lancaster County, in the State of Virginia, do certify that T. J. Downing, Special Commissioner, whose name is signed to the foregoing writing, bearing date on April 30 1912, has appeared before me, in my County aforesaid, and acknowledged the same. Given under my hand this 30th day of April, 1912 —

                 R. O. Norris Jr.
                 Com. in Chancery

Virginia:
In the Clerk's Office of the Circuit Court of Lancaster County the 24th day of April, 1914, this deed was presented and, with the certificate annexed, admitted to record at 4 o'clock P.M.
         Teste:

                 Wm. Chilton, Clerk

EXHIBIT 2-3

DEED BOOK 58, PAGE 119 — TO RAYMOND E. DOBYNS

Downing Sp. Com.
to
Dobyns
Apl. 30-12
May 1-12
80
$200.00
Chapel Dist
tax
1.75
1.00
2.75
[illegible]
1914

This deed, made and entered into this 30th day of April 1912, by and between T. J. Downing party of the first part and R. E. Dobyns, party of the second part witnesseth: that whereas the said T. J. Downing was appointed a Special Commissioner of the Circuit Court of Lancaster County, Virginia, by a decree pronounced by said Court in the Chancery cause therein depending on the 9th day of April 1912, which said Chancery cause was in the name and style of R. E. Dobyns et al vs. E. F. Haynie et als, by which said decree it was provided that the said R. E. Dobyns upon entering into and executing a note for the sum of Two hundred dollars, the payment of which was to be secured by a deed of trust on the land hereby to be conveyed, and other land should become the purchaser of that interest in the land formerly owned by Elnora B. Cox, to which the infant children of the said E. F. Haynie is entitled, as well as to the estate to which the said E. F. Haynie is entitled as tenant by Courtesy, all of which will more fully and at large appear from the proceedings in the suit above referred to, to which said suit reference is hereby made. Now this deed further witnesseth that for and in consideration that the said R. E. Dobyns has executed his certain note for the sum of Two hundred dollars, payable one year after date, with interest from date to the order of E. F. Haynie, guardian of Lewis F. Haynie, Elnora E. Haynie

EXHIBIT 2-4

McClinock B. Haynie + Nellie Haynie, and in the further consideration that the said R. E. Dobyns is ready and willing to execute the deed of trust in the said decree provided for. Now therefore the said F. J. Downing, Special Commissioner, as aforesaid has this day bargained and sold and by these presents does hereby bargain, sell, release and convey unto the said R. E. Dobyns all of the interest which accrued to the said E. F. Haynie by reason of his tenancy by the curtesy of Mamie C. Haynie, his deceased wife as well as all of the right, title and interest which was inherited by Lewis F. Haynie, Elnora E. Haynie, McClinock B. Haynie and Nellie Haynie from their mother the said Mamie C Haynie decd, in that tract of land said to contain eighty six acres, more or less, and which formerly belonged to Elnora E. Cox, which said land has this day been divided between the parties entitled thereto. The tract or parcel of land hereby conveyed is situated in White Chapel Magisterial district in Lancaster County, Va, and is supposed to contain three acres, and is bounded and described as follows:

The land hereby conveyed is with and adjoining the interest of Mrs. W. M. Streets and _____ heretofore conveyed, the said R. E. Dobyns, and for convenience, the two said interest viz: of the said Mrs Streets and the interest hereby conveyed will be described together — the two said interest thus lying together are bounded as follows: On the North by the la. of E. S. Dobyns and Mrs C. C. Chilton; on the East by the lands this day conveyed to Rosa E. Thomas and L. O. Cox on the South by the lands of L. O. Cox and the farm known as "Belmont", and on the West by the lands of E. S. Dobyns The eastern boundary is to be established between said R. E. Dobyns and Rosa E. Thomas as same is provided for in deed this day made by said F. J. Downing to said Ros. E. Thomas, to which said deed reference is hereby made.

To have and to hold the aforesaid tract or parcel of land to him the said R. E. Dobyns and his heirs and assigns forever. Witness the following hand and seal:

　　　　　　　　　　F. J. Downing　(Seal)
　　　　　　　　　　Special Commissioner

Erasures made before signing.

EXHIBIT 2-4

Virginia, Lancaster County, to-wit:

I, R. O. Norris Jr a Commissioner in Chancery of the Circuit Court for Lancaster County in the State of Virginia, do certify that F. J. Downing, Special Commissioner whose name is signed to the foregoing writing bearing date on April 30th 1912, has appeared before me in my said County and acknowledged the same. Given under my hand this 30th day of April 1912.

Virginia:

In the Clerk's Office of the Circuit Court of Lancaster County, the 1st day of May 1912, this deed was presented and, with the certificate annexed, admitted to record at 4 o'clock P.M.

Teste: L. R. Combs – Dp Clk

EXHIBIT 2-4

This deed, made and entered into this 30th day of April 1912 by and between R. E. Dobyns, party of the first part, and R. O. Norris Jr. party of the second part, witnesseth, that whereas the said R. E. Dobyns, party of the first part, is justly indebted to the trustee of the Glebe Fund of Lancaster County, in the just and full sum of Two Hundred and twenty seven and eighty eight cents ($227.88) which said debt is evidenced by the bond of the said R. E. Dobyns and E. S. Dobyns, and which said bond is payable twelve months after date, bearing interest from date, and the said R. E. Dobyns being now desirous to more effectually secure the payment of the said note, where the same shall fall due. Now therefore this deed witnesseth that for and in consideration of the sum of one dollar, cash in hand paid by the said R. O. Norris Jr. to the said R. E. Dobyns at and before the sealing and delivery of these presents, the receipt whereof is hereby acknowledged, the said R. E. Dobyns has this day bargained and sold, and by these presents does hereby bargain, sell, release and convey unto the said R. O. Norris Jr all of his right, title and interest in and to all of that certain tract or parcel of land lying and being in White Chapel Magisterial district in Lancaster County Va. which is said to contain forty three acres, be the same more or less, and which is bounded and described as follows: On the North by the lands of E. S. Dobyns & C. C. Chilton; on the South by the lands of L. O. Cox & farm known as "Belmont"; on the East by the lands of Rosa E. Thomas, and on the West by the lands of E. S. Dobyns. The land hereby conveyed is the same two interests of land acquired by the said R. E. Dobyns by deed from W. M. Street and wife, and by deed from T. J. Downing, Special Commissioner of the Circuit Court of Lancaster County, Va. To have and to hold the said land to him the said R. O. Norris Jr and his heirs and assigns forever with general warranty of title. In trust nevertheless for the following uses and purposes and none other, viz: that the said R. E. Dobyns shall remain in quiet and

DEED OF TRUST - R.E. DOBYNS TO R.O. NORRIS, JR. EXHIBIT 2-4

LEFT

This is a photograph of the 48 inch diameter pecan tree noted by Mr. Herbert P. Hall on his survey of July 3, 1911 as a "Small Pecan Tree".

RIGHT

This close-up of the H. P. Hall Pecan tree shows the three scars left by Mr. Hall's axe on July 3, 1911 to mark this as a boundary tree.
(The horizontal scars are faint in the old bark. They are circled in the photo with a black marking pen to assist in seeing them.)

EXHIBIT 2-5

Boggy area intended to be drained by the hand-dug ditch about 20 feet inside tree line to the left in picture. The ditch, dug sometime in the 1920's or early 1930's, is now partially filled in and not efficient in draining the area.

The hand-dug ditch is visible in the middle of the picture, with the cut poplar tree in the background on the left side of the ditch. This tree was marked as a boundary tree before being cut by DFLLC loggers in the summer of 2013.

EXHIBIT 2-6

By CHARLES R. PRUETT, CLS

EXHIBIT 2-7

This deed made this 25th day of February in the year 1874 between John R. Chilton of Lancaster County, Virginia and Cornelia his wife of the one part and Sarah Tomlin of Lancaster County, Virginia of the other part. Witnesseth that the said John R. Chilton and Cornelia his wife for and in Consideration of the sum of One Hundred and forty eight 50/100 dollars good and lawful money of the United States to them in hand paid by the said Sarah Tomlin at or before the sealing and delivery of these presents the receipt whereof they do hereby acknowledge and thereof acquit and forever discharge the said Sarah Tomlin her heirs executors and administrators by these presents have sold, granted, aliened enfeoffed released and confirmed unto the said Sarah Tomlin and unto his heirs and assigns forever ten lots or pieces of land Situated in the County of Lancaster State of Virginia and containing in the aggregate sixteen and four fifth Acres Bounded and described as follows to wit the first one lot beginning at a corner of ___ the lands of the said Sarah Tomlin and running S ___ 40.4.38 chains to J. R. Chilton's lines thence with them N 55 ½° W 6.95 chains N 30 ½° W 95 links thence with Henry Lowry N 33 ½° W 5.40 chains to Frances Tomlin's line, thence with them N 18 ½° E 3.35 chains, thence with him S 55 ½° E 5.20 chains with Rosilvent Tomlin S 53½° E 6.45 chains to the beginning.

The lot of four and four fifths acres beginning at a corner with Henry Lowry and running S 39 ½° W 17.60 chains to J. R. Chilton's line thence with him N 2 ½° W 2.90 chains to Richmond Coleman's line, thence with him N 39 ½° E 17.20 chains thence S 33 ½° E 7.80 chains to the beginning.

To have and to hold the said lots or pieces of land with the appurtenances unto the said Sarah Tomlin her heirs and assigns forever, And the said John R. Chilton for himself his heirs, executors and administrators for and in behalf of the said Cornelia his wife and her heirs the covenant, promise and agree to and with the said Sarah Tomlin her heirs and assigns forever to these presents ___

EXHIBIT 3-1

in manner and form following to wit. That he the said John R. Chilton and his heirs the said lots or piece of land and premises hereby granted or intended so to be with appurtenances unto the said Noah Lowden his heirs and assigns against him the said John R. Chilton and his heirs and against the heirs of the said Cornelia his wife and against all and every person or persons whatsoever will warrant and forever defend by these presents. In witness whereof we have hereunto set our hands and seals this 21st day of Feby 1874

J. R. Chilton (Seal)

Cornelia C. Chilton (Seal)

Lancaster County to wit:

I W. S. Smead a justice of the peace for the county afore-said in the State of Virginia do certify that John R. Chilton whose name is signed to the writing above bearing date on the 21st day of Feby 1874 has acknowledged the same before me in my county aforesaid Given under my hand this 21st day of February 1874

W. S. Smead JP.

Lancaster County to wit:

We Wm S. Smead and Thomas B Robinson justices of the peace for the County of Lancaster in the State of Virginia do certify that Cornelia the wife of John R Chilton whose name are signed to the writing above bearing date on the 21st day of February 1874 personally appeared before us in the County aforesaid and being examined by us privily and apart from her husband and having the writing aforesaid fully explained to her She the said Cornelia acknowledged the said writing to be her act and declared that she had willingly executed the same and does not wish to retract it.

Given under our hands this 21st day of Feby. Anno Domini 1874.

W. S. Smead JP.

Thos B Robinson JP.

Office of the Clerk of the County Court of Lancaster March 12. 1875 This deed from John R. Chilton and wife to Noah Lowden was received in the office aforesaid and together with the certificate thereto annexed admitted to record

Teste

Warner [____]

EXHIBIT 3-1

– 122 –

This Deed made this 9th day of October, 1911, between Masten Toulin, sr. of Nuluck, Lancaster county, Virginia, party of the first part, and Ada Jackson, nee Toulin, of the same place, daughter of the said Masten Toulin, sr. party of the second part.

Witnesseth: that in consideration of the sum of $1.00, and for the natural love and affection which he the said Masten Toulin has unto the said Ada Jackson, nee Toulin, his daughter, the said Masten Toulin, sr. by these presents does give, grant, alien, convey and confirm unto the said Ada Jackson, nee Toulin, her heirs and assigns forever, all that certain tract of land said to contain four acres by estimation, let it be more or less, together with a small dwelling house thereon, situated near Nuluck, in the county of Lancaster and state of Virginia; and bounded as follows, to wit; commencing at the centre of Seerins creek with the land of J. O. Cox, thence in a westerly direction along with the land of the said J. O. Cox, to a large white Oak tree east of the house, thence along with same land to a holly tree marked as a corner line, thence in a westerly direction along with the land of the late John R. Clifton 100 yards, to a cedar stake, thence in a northerly direction by the centre of the said creek, thence down the centre of said creek to the beginning point, the same being the residence of the said Masten Toulin and where he now resides, and was conveyed to him by his father the late Noah Toulin, sr. the said Masten Toulin, sr. reserves a house as long as he lives in and upon the said premises with the said Ada Jackson, nee Toulin, the said Masten Toulin, sr. party of the first part covenant that he has the right to convey the said land to the grantee; that he has done no act to encumber the said land; that the grantee shall have quiet possession of the said land free from encumbrances and the said Masten Toulin, sr. party of the first part will execute such further assurance of the said land as may be requisite. Witness the following signature and seal.

— Masten Toulin, sr. (Seal)

EXHIBIT 3-2

State of Virginia; Lancaster County, Towit;

I, L. H. A. Flemings, a justice of the peace for the county aforesaid, in the state of Virginia; do certify that Martin Towler, at whose name is signed to the within writing bearing date on the 9th day of October, 1911 has acknowledged the same before me in my county aforesaid. Given under my hand this 19th day of October 1911.

L. A. Flemings J. P. (Seal)

Virginia:

In the clerk's office of the circuit court for the county of Lancaster, the 3rd day of July, 1912, This deed was presented and, with the certificate annexed, admitted to record at 9 o'clock, a. m.

Teste:

Wm Chilton, Clerk.

EXHIBIT 3-2

MOTON TOMLIN, SR. TO DAUGHTER MARY EULINE JONES

This deed made this 9th day of October, 1911, between Moton Tomlin, Sr., of Molusk, Lancaster County, Virginia, party of the first part and Mary Euline Jones nee Tomlin, of the same place, daughter of the said Moton Tomlin, Sr., party of the second part:

WITNESSETH: That in consideration of the sum of one dollar and for the natural love and affection which he the said Moton Tomlin, Sr., has unto the said Mary Euline Jones nee Tomlin, his daughter, the said Moton Tomlin, Sr., by these presents, does give, grant, alien, convey and confirm unto the said Mary Euline Jones nee Tomlin, her heirs and assigns, forever, all that certain tract of land, said to contain three acres by estimation, let it be more or less, situated near Molusk, in the county of Lancaster and state of Virginia and bounded as follows, towit: Commencing at a cedar stob at the cor. of Ada Jackson's land, thence in a westerly direction along with the land of John R. Chilton, decd., to the center of a swamp to the land of Richmond Coleman, thence down the center of the said swamp to the center of head of Seenius Creek, thence down the center of the said creek to the land of Ada Jackson, thence in a southerly direction to the said cedar stob at the beginning point, the same being the remainder of the tract of land of the said Moton Tomlin, Sr., after deeding Ada Jackson nee Tomlin four acres of his home place, which was deeded to him by his father, the late Noah Tomlin, Sr. The said Moton Tomlin, Sr., covenants that he has the right to convey the said land to the grantee, that he has done no act to encumber the said land, that the grantee shall have quiet possession of the said land, free from all encumbrances and that said Moton Tomlin, Sr., party of the first part will execute such further assurance of the said land as may be requisite. Witness the following signature and seel:

Moton Tomlin, Sr.   (Seal)

State of Virginia, Lancaster County, towit:
I, L. R. Flemings, a Justice of the Peace for the county aforesaid, in the state of Virginia, do certify that Moton Tomlin, Sr., whose name is signed to the within writing, bearing date on the 9th, day of October, 1911, has acknowledged the same before me in my county aforesaid.
Given under my hand this 19th, day of October, 1911.
L. R. Flemings, J. P.   (Seal)

Virginia, towit:
In the Clerk's Office of the Circuit Court of Lancaster County, the 3rd. day of March, 1919, this deed was presented and with the certificate annext, admitted to record at 9 o'clock, A. M.
Teste:
Oscar B. Chilton Dep. Clerk

EXHIBIT 3-3

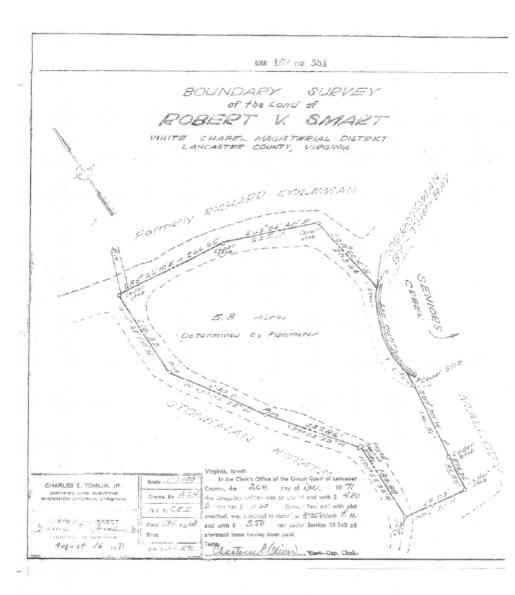

BOUNDARY SURVEY
of the Land of

ROBERT V. SMART

WHITE CHAPEL MAGISTERIAL DISTRICT
LANCASTER COUNTY, VIRGINIA

5.8 Acres
Determined by Planimeter

CHARLES E. TOMLIN, JR.
CERTIFIED LAND SURVEYOR
WICOMICO CHURCH, VIRGINIA

August 16 1971

Virginia, to-wit:
In the Clerk's Office of the Circuit Court of Lancaster County, the 20th day of Dec., 19 71 the foregoing writing was presented and with $ 4.20 in state Tax $ 1.60 County Tax and with plat attached, was admitted to record at 3:25 o'clock P. M. and with $ 5.50 tax under Section 58.54B all aforesaid taxes having been paid.

EXHIBIT 4-1

Mrs. Edward J. Novak
272 Ostrich Drive
Galion, Ohio 44833

Aug. 1, 1975

Dear Bob,

I hope you don't mind if I call you that. Fresh thought so much of you and your family, and talked so much about you all, that we feel we know you.

Thank you for your nice note. I'm very glad that someone bought "our piece of Virginia" that really appreciates Virginia.

We are planning a trip home about Aug. 11th we will spend part of the time in King William with my sister, and part of the time in Warsaw. If you and your wife are going by and see an Ohio car in the drive, please stop. We'd like very much to meet you both.

Sincerely,
Bennie Novak

P.S. I only use the name Olga legally!!

EXHIBIT 5-1

The top photo shows the corner of the fence at Point A. The white PVC pipe, with blue survey tape, marks the actual location where the stone was buried. The old, graveled Smart Family driveway can be seen just to the **north** of the PVC pipe.

The bottom photo looks in the opposite direction from the photo above. The photo shows the location of the Cox Family home (single story portion of the house) in relation to where the stone was buried (corner of the fence) by Mr. Dobyns, Mr. Cox, and his daughter, Mrs. Thomas, in 1912.

EXHIBIT 5-2

RIGHT OF WAY SURVEY

ROBERT V. SMART

WHITE CHAPEL MAGISTERIAL DISTRICT
LANCASTER COUNTY, VIRGINIA

SMART

DOBYNS

PD STONE

22

PIPE

N 75° 30'00" E 256.00'

0.14 Ac.

215.00'

234.00'

S 75° 30'00" W 256.00'

BARTLETT

POWER POLE

PIPE

19.00'

END OF STATE MAINTENANCE

PIPE

VSH 662

SCALE _____ 1" = 50'

CERTIFIED CORRECT	TOMLIN & KEYSER	DRAWN BY H.B.H	FIELD 231 PG 20
	CERTIFIED LAND SURVEYORS		BOOK _____ PG _____
FIELD LAND SURVEYOR	WICOMICO CHURCH, VIRGINIA.	CK'D BY R.H.PL	H.C. _____
July 13, 1973		JOB NO. LC324	REV. DATE _____

EXHIBIT 5-3

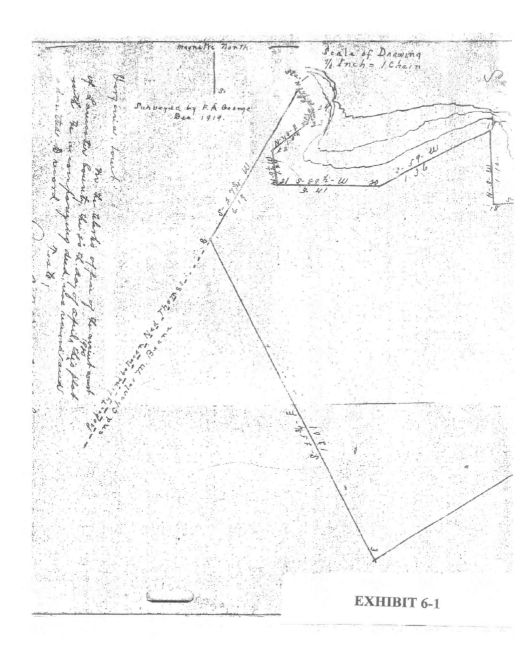

EXHIBIT 6-1

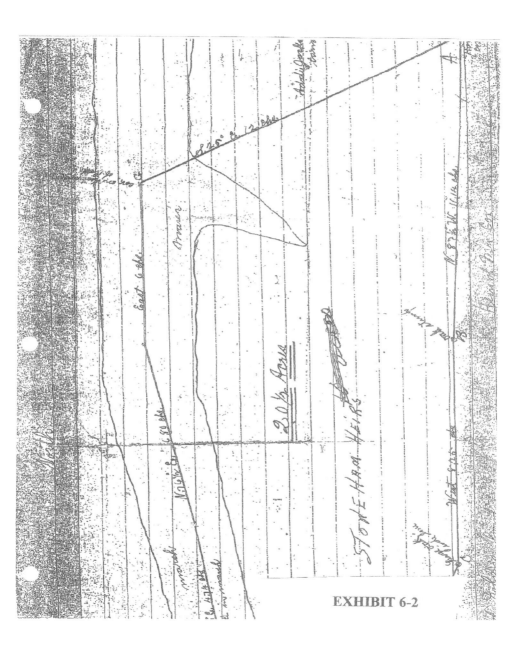

EXHIBIT 6-2

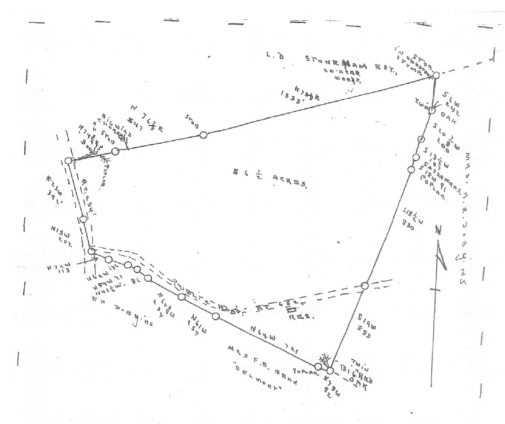

Survey of 56.50 acres located in Lancaster Co. Va. Near Molusk.
belonging to Thomas A. Dobyns and E.L. Dobyns.

Jan 17 1951 .

Mag. Mer.

Scale 300 ft. to 1 inch.

T. H. Warner
T.H.Warner
State Certified Surveyor
Tappahannock Va.

EXHIBIT 6-3

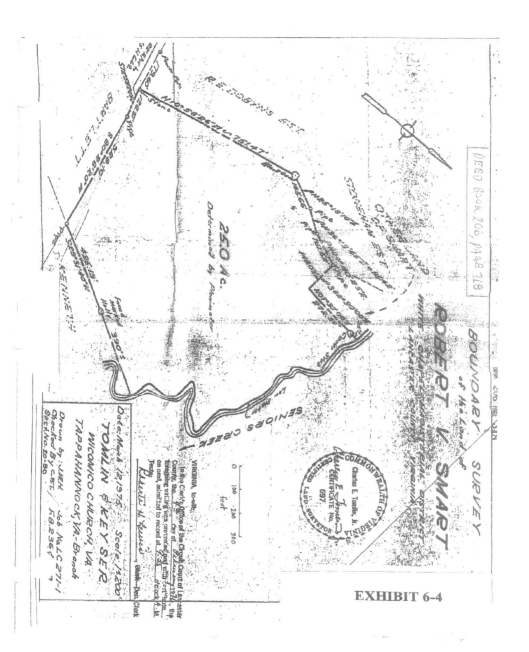

EXHIBIT 6-4

– 133 –

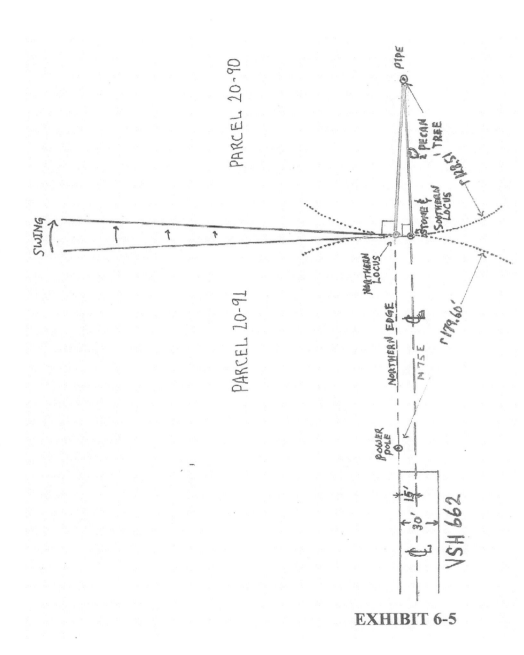

EXHIBIT 6-5

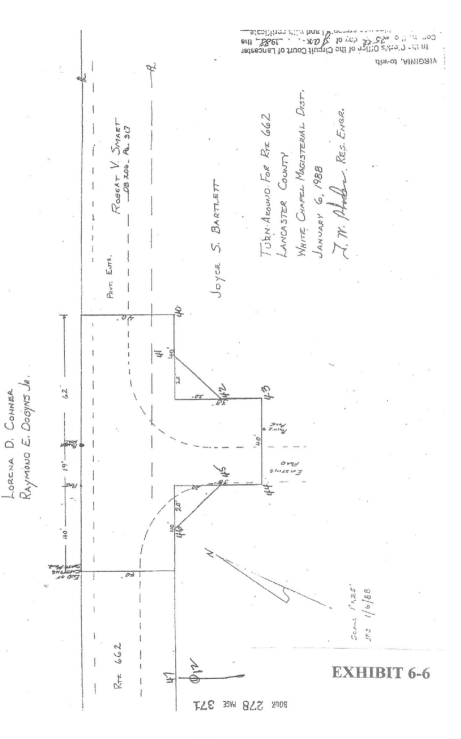

EXHIBIT 6-6

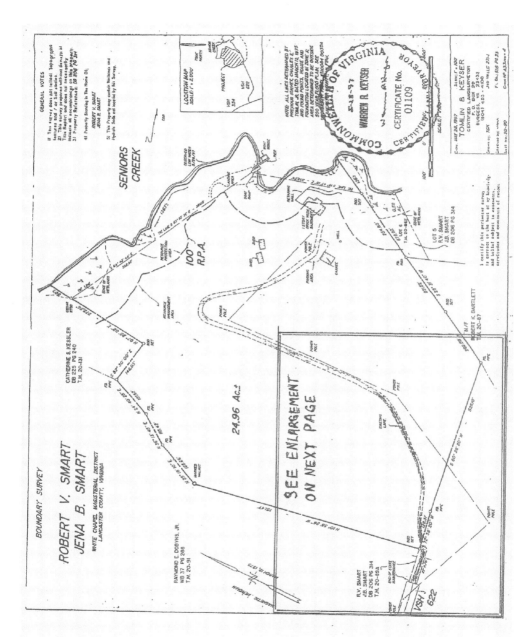

EXHIBIT 6-7

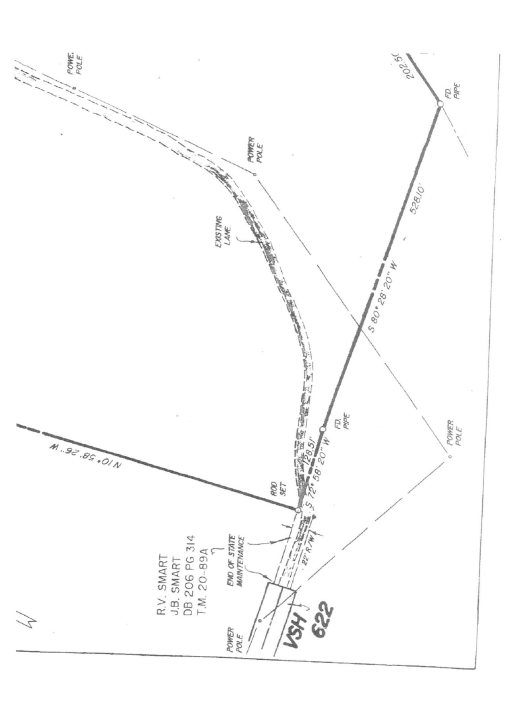

R.V. SMART
J.B. SMART
DB 206 PG 314
T.M. 20-89A

POWER POLE

POWER POLE

POWER POLE

POWER POLE

EXISTING LANE.

ROD SET

FD. PIPE

FD. PIPE

END OF STATE MAINTENANCE

N 10° 58' 26" W

S 72° 58' 20" W

128.5'

22' R/W

S 80° 28' 20" W

528.10'

202.5

VSH 622

EXHIBIT 6-8

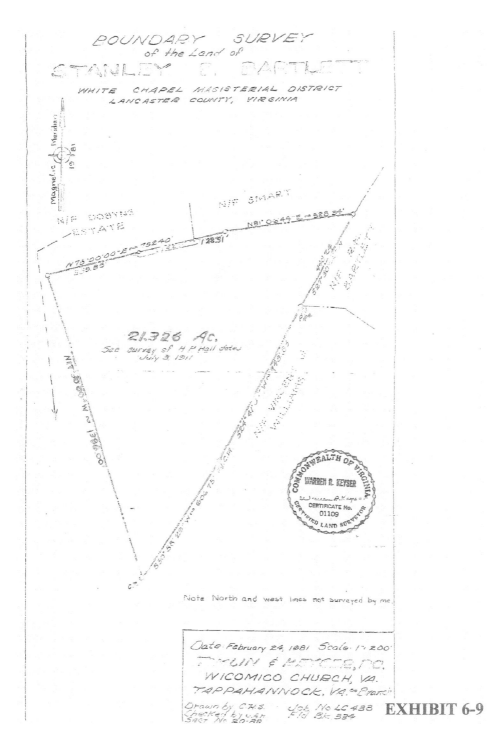

BOUNDARY SURVEY
of the Land of
STANLEY G. BARTLETT
WHITE CHAPEL MAGISTERIAL DISTRICT
LANCASTER COUNTY, VIRGINIA

21.326 Ac.
See survey of H P Hall dated
July 3, 1911

Note North and west lines not surveyed by me.

COMMONWEALTH OF VIRGINIA
WARREN R. KEYSER
CERTIFICATE No.
01109
CERTIFIED LAND SURVEYOR

Date February 24, 1981 Scale 1"-200'
MARLIN & ASSOCIATES, INC.
WICOMICO CHURCH, VA.
TAPPAHANNOCK, VA. Branch

Drawn by C.H.S.
Checked by J.S.M.
Sheet No. 20-AD
Job No LC 438
Fld Bk 334

EXHIBIT 6-9

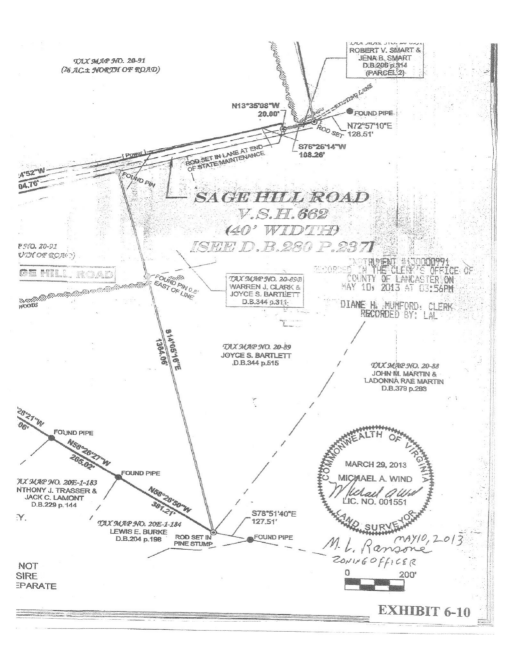

TAX MAP NO. 20-91
(26 AC.± NORTH OF ROAD)

ROBERT V. SMART &
JENA B. SMART
D.B.206 p.314
(PARCEL 2)

N13°35'08"W
20.00'

FOUND PIPE

N72°57'10"E
128.51'

ROD SET

S76°26'14"W
108.26'

ROD SET IN LANE AT END
OF STATE MAINTENANCE

4°52"W
04.76'

FOUND PIN

[Power]

SAGE HILL ROAD
V.S.H.662
(40' WIDTH
[SEE D.B.280 P.237]

P NO. 20-91
U N OF ROAD)

GE HILL ROAD

WOODS

FOUND PIN 0.8'
EAST OF LINE

TAX MAP NO. 20-89B
WARREN J. CLARK &
JOYCE S. BARTLETT
D.B.344 p.311:

INSTRUMENT #130000791
RECORDED IN THE CLERK'S OFFICE OF
COUNTY OF LANCASTER ON
MAY 10, 2013 AT 03:56PM

DIANE H. MUMFORD, CLERK
RECORDED BY: LAL

S14°05'16"E
1364.06'

TAX MAP NO. 20-89
JOYCE S. BARTLETT
D.B.344 p.515

TAX MAP NO. 20-88
JOHN M. MARTIN &
LADONNA RAE MARTIN
D.B.379 p.293

28'21"W
06'

FOUND PIPE

N58°26'27"W
285.02'

FOUND PIPE

AX MAP NO. 20E-1-183
NTHONY J. TRASSER &
JACK C. LAMONT
D.B.229 p.144

N58°28'50"W
381.21'

TAX MAP NO. 20E-1-184
LEWIS E. BURKE
D.B.204 p.198

ROD SET IN
PINE STUMP

S78°51'40"E
127.51'

FOUND PIPE

COMMONWEALTH OF VIRGINIA
MARCH 29, 2013
MICHAEL A. WIND
Michael A. Wind
LIC. NO. 001551
LAND SURVEYOR

M. L. Ransone
ZONING OFFICER

MAY 10, 2013

NOT
SIRE
EPARATE

0   200'

EXHIBIT 6-10

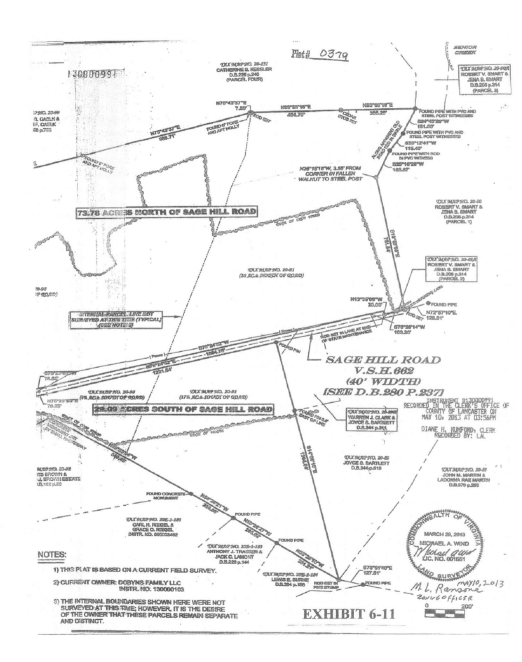

Plat # 0379

EXHIBIT 6-11

NOTES:

1) THIS PLAT IS BASED ON A CURRENT FIELD SURVEY.

2) CURRENT OWNER: DOBYNS FAMILY LLC
   INSTR. NO. 130000103

3) THE INTERNAL BOUNDARIES SHOWN HERE WERE NOT
   SURVEYED AT THIS TIME; HOWEVER, IT IS THE DESIRE
   OF THE OWNER THAT THESE PARCELS REMAIN SEPARATE
   AND DISTINCT.

SAGE HILL ROAD
V.S.H. 662
(40' WIDTH)
[SEE D.B. 280 P.237]

73.78 ACRES NORTH OF SAGE HILL ROAD

29.09 ACRES SOUTH OF SAGE HILL ROAD

TOP

Dense thicket of vines in the boggy area along Line "A-F". This is why my father and I never measured the 751.47 feet from SW corner to the black gum tree.

BOTTOM

Cedar stob placed by Mr. Wind where Parcels 20-90, 20-91 and 20-131 would come together if the boundary line between Parcels 20-90 and 20-91 had been drawn according to Mr. H. P. Hall's survey and Mr. T. J. Downing's deed.

EXHIBIT 6-12

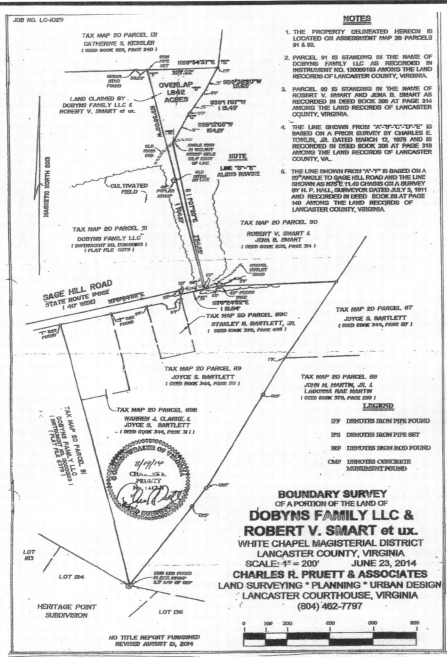

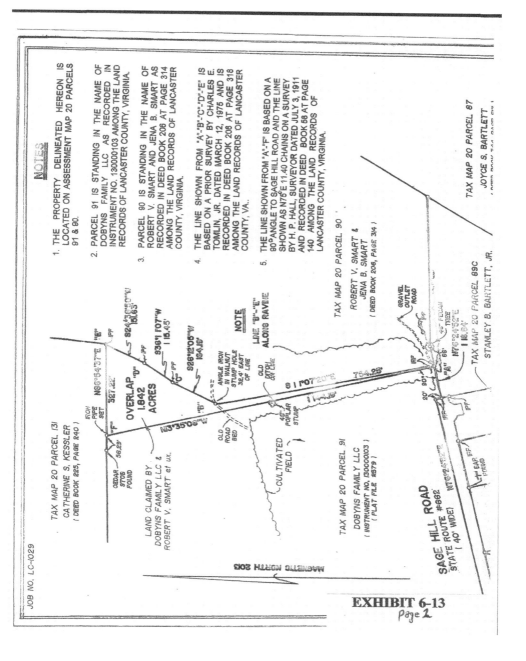

NOTES

1. THE PROPERTY DELINEATED HEREON IS LOCATED ON ASSESSMENT MAP 20 PARCELS 91 & 90.

2. PARCEL 91 IS STANDING IN THE NAME OF DOBYNS FAMILY LLC AS RECORDED IN INSTRUMENT NO. 130000103 AMONG THE LAND RECORDS OF LANCASTER COUNTY, VIRGINIA.

3. PARCEL 90 IS STANDING IN THE NAME OF ROBERT V. SMART AND JENA B. SMART AS RECORDED IN DEED BOOK 206 AT PAGE 314 AMONG THE LAND RECORDS OF LANCASTER COUNTY, VIRGINIA.

4. THE LINE SHOWN FROM "A"-"B"-"C"-"D"-"E" IS BASED ON A PRIOR SURVEY BY CHARLES E. TOMLIN, JR. DATED MARCH 12, 1975 AND IS RECORDED IN DEED BOOK 208 AT PAGE 318 AMONG THE LAND RECORDS OF LANCASTER COUNTY, VA.

5. THE LINE SHOWN FROM "A"-"F" IS BASED ON A 90° ANGLE TO SAGE HILL ROAD AND THE LINE SHOWN AS N75°E 11.40 CHAINS ON A SURVEY BY H. P. HALL, SURVEYOR DATED JULY 3, 1911 AND RECORDED IN DEED BOOK 58 AT PAGE 140 AMONG THE LAND RECORDS OF LANCASTER COUNTY, VIRGINIA.

JOB NO. LC-1029

TAX MAP 20 PARCEL 131
CATHERINE S. KESSLER
(DEED BOOK 225, PAGE 240)

TAX MAP 20 PARCEL 90
ROBERT V. SMART &
JENA B. SMART
(DEED BOOK 206, PAGE 314)

TAX MAP 20 PARCEL 87
JOYCE S. BARTLETT

TAX MAP 20 PARCEL 89C
STANLEY B. BARTLETT, JR.

TAX MAP 20 PARCEL 91
DOBYNS FAMILY LLC
(INSTRUMENT NO. 130000103)
(PLAT FILE K579)

LAND CLAIMED BY
DOBYNS FAMILY LLC &
ROBERT V. SMART et ux.

OVERLAP
1.842
ACRES

NOTE
LINE "B"-"E"
ALONG RAVINE

CULTIVATED
FIELD

SAGE HILL ROAD
#662
STATE ROUTE
(40' WIDE)

MAGNETIC NORTH 2013

EXHIBIT 6-13
Page 2

- 143 -

525 Colinbrook Way
Lancaster, VA 22503-2622
May 10, 2013

Mr. and Mrs. Robert V. Smart
P.O. Box 160
Mollusk, VA 22517

Dear Mr. and Mrs. Smart,

As you know, we have recently had Michael A. Wind, Certified Land Surveyor, survey the Dobyns Family LLC property bordering Sage Hill Road in White Chapel Magisterial District, Lancaster County, VA. as the first step in harvesting timber on our property. We plan to file the aforementioned survey at the Lancaster County Courthouse no later than May 13, 2013. We understand you now have issues with the line which borders your property at the end of Sage Hill Road. The property line with which you have issues is exactly the same as is on a survey of your property which you recorded on the 4th day of February, 1976 in Lancaster County. The line is, of course, the same which you walked with my uncle, Raymond E. Dobyns, Jr., my husband, and me within the past two years when you kindly offered to show us the boundary between the Dobyns land and yours which you have maintained over many years with white PVC pipes at points where bearings change.

We are confident that the line that you showed us and as depicted on the Wind survey is the correct property line. We have signed a contract for timber harvesting on the entire Dobyns Family LLC tract, and we understand initial cutting could be imminent, but likely would not occur within two weeks. In light of the issues regarding the line which you have only very recently raised, and which we deem unwarranted, we wanted you to be on notice of our intentions.

Sincerely,

Anita Conner Tadlock

Anita Conner Tadlock, Manager
Dobyns Family LLC

EXHIBIT 6-14

– 144 –

Mrs. Anita Conner Tadlock
Manager, Dobyns Family LLC
525 Colinbrook Way
Lancaster, VA 22503-2622

Dear Anita,

After receiving your letter, Jena and I feel it is good to write to you. Since the beginning of Mr. Michael Wind's survey, Jena and I have learned a great deal. In the last few weeks, Bob has spent hours in the land records office, verifying marks in the field, and studying our records and family photo albums. As Jena and I recount what we have learned, please forgive the blending of our family history into the narrative. This technique has helped us to understand the timeline of events spanning many decades.

In 1969 Bob returned home from his second tour in Vietnam and spent a week with his parents, Don and Ocie, at their small vacation home in the new Corrotoman By The Bay (CBTB) development. During that week, Bob fell in love with this area. Its tranquility was the antithesis of the turmoil in Vietnam. By the end of the week, Bob had decided to buy land in this area with the thought of retiring here – a distant dream for a 25 year old Navy lieutenant. On May 3, 1973 Bob bought a tract of land from a wonderful lady named Margaret Thomas Mallory. In early 1975, Bob's parents retired. They were planning to move to this area, but Ocie did not want the small CBTB vacation home to become their retirement abode. About the same time, Bob returned from a tour in Senegal and again visited his parents. It was during that visit he suggested his parents build a home on the land he had recently purchased from Margaret T. Mallory. Mom and dad thought it was a great idea and dad began work on it immediately.

Margaret Mallory's mother was Mrs. Rosa E. Thomas. Margaret acquired the property from her. Rosa Thomas had acquired the land from Mrs. Elnora Cox in an undisputed settlement among Elnora's heirs after she passed away. The settlement was executed by a specially appointed commissioner, the well known Mr. T. J. Downing. On April 30, 1912, Mr. Downing worked on the deeds of conveyance to execute the settlement. First, he drafted the deed of conveyance for land adjoining Rosa's land to the south. Mr. Downing wrote that deed to Mr. Louis O. Cox. A survey of Mr. Cox's land had been done by Mr. H. P. Hall on July 3, 1911, and Mr. Downing included that survey as part of the deed to Mr. L. O. Cox. Later that same day, Mr. Downing wrote the deed of conveyance for Rosa E. Thomas, see Attachment One. In Rosa's deed he referenced the Hall, 1911 survey when he described the western boundary of her land. Regarding that boundary, Mr. Downing wrote that it was to run to the land owned by Mrs. C. C. Chilton (now owned by Mrs. Catherine S. Kessler, recorded at D.B.225 p.240, Parcel Four). By the description given, the boundary was to run at right angles to a line of the Hall, 1911 survey, see Attachment Two. The point of origination where the boundary line was to be turned was to be determined. Some time after April 30, 1912, the point of

EXHIBIT 6-15
P. 1

origination (turning point for the westward boundary line) was determined and a stone was buried at that point.

In March 1975, I hired Tomlin and Keyser, certified land surveyors (CLS) to survey the property which I had purchased from Mrs. Mallory so that my father could build on my land. The survey was done by Mr. Charles E. Tomlin, Jr., CLS #697, and certified by him on March 12, 1975. The plat of the survey was filed in the Lancaster Courthouse on February 4, 1976. Only in the last four weeks have Jena and I known about the gross inaccuracy of the survey. Mr. Tomlin failed to follow the description in deed of the property he was surveying. As a result, he excluded approximately three acres from the tract. Some time after the southwest corner stone was identified on the survey, it was removed.

Jena and I were married on April 26, 1975. Construction was completed on my parent's home by July 4, 1976, and Jena and I were able to join our extended family for a wonderful bicentennial celebration at the new home.

Mr. Tomlin passed away many years ago, so we will never know why he ignored Mr. Downing's description of the property he was surveying. It is evident Mr. Tomlin used the Hall, 1911 survey for the southern boundary. He located the buried stone and gives bearings and distances from it to other marks. Beginning at the point of origination (the stone), he completely ignores the description of the property he was surveying. He did not turn a right angle as called for in the deed; he turned an angle of 83 degrees, 56 minutes, 46 seconds, missing a right angle by over six degrees. He did not go to the land once owned by Mrs. C. C. Chilton. Instead, he wandered down a swale and completely missed a common boundary with Mrs. Chilton's land. On the southern boundary, Mr. Tomlin labels two lines of the Hall, 1911 survey with bearings which properly indicate an inflection of 7 degrees, 30 minutes. But he then draws the plat for his own survey with a five degree inflection. This creates the optical illusion that the westward boundary is drawn two and one-half degrees closer to a right angle. In addition, two statements made by Mr. Tomlin in his Surveyor's Report regarding the westward boundary are not true. All of this went unknown by Jena and me for 38 years. During this time, my parents passed away, Jena and I raised our family, and I completed a thirty year career in the service at duty stations around the world. In short, life got in the way of a close comparison of deed to survey. On April 26, 2013, while searching land records related to our right-of-way, Bob discovered the problem. Two days later, Jena and I made an appointment to meet with Mr. Wind at his Tappahannock, VA office. That meeting took place on Tuesday, May 7, 2013. On Monday, May 13, 2013, we received your certified letter.

As mentioned, Bob began research at the land record office when Mr. Wind's survey stake appeared in the right-of-way which my family has used for 38 years. In 1973, Bob had purchased a 22 foot wide right-of-way from the Bartlett Family to get from VSH 662 to the southwest corner of the land he had just purchased. That distance is now 108.26 feet. (It used to be a greater distance before the state acquired additional right-of-way to create a school bus turn-around.) Bob hired Tomlin and Keyser, CLS, to survey the

EXHIBIT 6-15
P. 2

purchased right-of-way. The survey was done on July 13, 1973. It shows the right-of-way with its northern edge in straight alignment with the northern edge of VSH 662, through the power pole to the buried stone, see <u>Attachment Three.</u> In the last four weeks, Jena and I have also learned that this survey is also grossly inaccurate. When Mr. Wind's stake showing the location of the missing stone appeared in the right-of-way, Bob at first rejected the accuracy of that location. But after personally verifying distances and bearings, and after verifying with the power company that power pole (R2-229-7L) had not been moved since placement in 1971, Bob concluded that the stake was accurately placed to mark the location of the missing stone. Bob also verified that the stake lies on the N75E leg of the Hall, 1911 survey. Accepting the location of the stake as the location of the missing stone led to the discovery by Jena and Bob that 5/100ths of an acre (108.26 feet X 20 feet = 2,165.2 square feet divided by 43,560 square feet per acre) of the right-of-way does not belong to us. In 1973, when Bob filed the right-of-way survey in Lancaster Courthouse, it began an unfortunate tradition of trusting certified land surveys by Tomlin and Keyser.

The land area lying to the east of the boundary line specified by Mr. Downing ("Downing Line") and lying to the west of the line invented by Mr. Tomlin ("Tomlin, 1975") is about 3 acres, see <u>Attachment Four.</u> The Downing Deed to Mrs. Rosa E. Thomas was written 63 years before the erroneous Tomlin survey was done. Jena and I hold the deed assigning those three acres to Mrs. Rosa E. Thomas by special commissioner T.J. Downing.

I have tried to act in good faith and as a good neighbor, maintaining marks and showing them to you when you asked. Only recently have I learned that I was acting in ignorance, having been deceived by a faulty survey – one inconsistent with true documents.

We recognize that as manager of Dobyns Family LLC, you have to make tough decisions. And we know that some of these decisions may pit business interests against what you may feel is right. We ask you to consider that Jena and I had unclouded title to the three acres in question when we were married on April 26, 1975, before the faulty Tomlin survey was filed. And we have done nothing knowingly to cloud that title. About a month ago, in conversation regarding the placement of the stake in what we thought was our purchased right-of-way, you said that you just wanted the line to go where it is supposed to go. You were right. Jena and I are incredulous at the "twists and turns" of the last month. Now we are in the position of asking you for the line to go where it is supposed to go. As a professional, Mr. Tomlin did not do his job, and Mr. Downing is "turning over in his grave". Jena and I humbly ask you to request Mr. Wind to draw his plat to honor our deed. We will then have a surveyor survey that boundary in accordance with our deed. When both surveys, by adjoining landowners, are filed in Lancaster Courthouse, the error created by Mr. Tomlin is corrected. It would be a remarkable story to finally put into effect, after 101 years, an amicable settlement executed by Mr. T.J. Downing and notarized by Mr. Robert O. Norris, Jr. The sinking of the <u>Titanic</u> had occurred just two weeks before Mr. Downing executed his amicable division among Mr. Raymond.E. Dobyns, Mr. Louis O. Cox, and Mrs. Rosa E. Thomas.

EXHIBIT 6-15
P. 3

It seems that time accelerates as we grow older, and every hour certainly brings us closer to the final destination. Soon enough the next generation of your family and ours will be neighbors. Jena and I pray that life will be as wonderful for all of them as it has been for us.

With Christian Love,

Jena & Bob

EXHIBIT 6-15
P. 4

– 148 –

525 Colinbrook Way
Lancaster, Virginia 22503-2622

May 28, 2013

Mr. and Mrs. Robert V. Smart
P.O. Box 160
Mollusk, VA 22517

Dear Mr. and Mrs. Smart,

We have conferred with counsel, and we believe that our position regarding the disputed parcel is sound. We are going to proceed accordingly.

Very truly yours,

Anita Conner Tadlock

Anita Conner Tadlock, Manager
Dobyns Family LLC

EXHIBIT 6-16

June 1, 2013

Mrs. Anita Conner Tadlock
Manager, Dobyns Family LLC
525 Colinbrook Way
Lancaster, VA 22503-2622

Dear Mrs. Tadlock,

I am advised to inform you that we hold title to the disputed parcel, and the dispute has not been resolved in your favor. If you proceed with logging across the "Downing Line" prior to resolution, it may cost Dobyns Family LLC more than the value of the timber.

Sincerely,

Robert V. Avrot

EXHIBIT 6-17

This photo shows the new DFLLC fence on centerline at the end of Sage
Hill Road, with reflectors to keep people from running into it at night. The
repositioned Smart Family driveway runs to the south of the fence, as a
direct extension off the right hand side of Sage Hill Road. The giant forked
tree in the background is 66 feet (one chain) from the far corner of the fence.
That huge tree is the "small pecan tree" noted on Mr. H. P. Hall's survey of
July 3, 1911.

EXHIBIT 6-18

CAREER TRAINING LIST

NOAA

LINEAL#	LNAME	FNAME	DATE	CODE	TYP	TITLE
13.00	Smart	Robert	4-Feb-94	4	ST	INTRO TO WINDOWS 3.1
			10-Nov-93	4	ST	NOAA EEO CONFERENCE
			25-Oct-93	4	ST	PREVENTING SEXUAL HARASSMENT
			13-Jan-93	4	ST	DIFFERENTIAL GPS ←
			7-Jan-93	4	ST	PMC COMMAND SEMINAR
			22-Jul-92	4	ST	SMALL PURCHASES
			10-Feb-92	4	ST	TOTAL QUALITY MANAGEMENT
			7-Jan-92	4	ST	MARINE COMMAND SEMINAR
			31-Dec-91	4	CC	SMALL PURCHASE/FED.SUPPLYSCHED
			3-May-91	4	CC	NAVIGATIONAL RULES
			26-Apr-91	4	ST	DAMAGE CONTROL/FIRE FIGHTING
			26-Oct-90	4	ST	BUDGET/FINANCIAL MANAGEMENT
			16-Mar-90	4	ST	IMMERSIONINTENSIVESPANISHINST.
			27-Jun-89	4	ST	INTRODUCTORY WORDPERFECT 5.0
			12-May-89	3	ST	PROGRAM PLANNING & ANALYSI
			8-Jun-87	4	ST	PERFORMANCE MANAGEMENT
			1-May-87	4	ST	DOC EXECUTIVE FORUM FY87
			10-Mar-87	4	ST	MANAGING EXCELLENCE SEMINAR
			24-Jan-85	4	ST	PERFORMANCE STANDARDS WORKS
			18-Jan-85	4	ST	XO WORKSHOP ON DISCIPLINE
			18-Sep-84	4	ST	MARINE FIREFIGHTING COURSE
			12-Sep-84	4	ST	MARINE DAMAGE CONTROL
			1-Sep-84	4	CC	RULES OF THE ROAD
			24-Jun-83	4	ST	COLLEGE OF NAVAL WARFARE
			24-Sep-81	4	ST	CAPITOL HILL WORKSHOP
			16-Jul-81	4	ST	WORKFORCE PERF. APPRAISAL
			12-May-81	4	ST	MERIT PAY PERF APPRAISAL SYS.
			1-Apr-81	4	ST	PROJECT MANAGEMENT
			18-Jan-80	4	ST	ARMED FORCES STAFF COLLEGE
			12-Jan-79	4	ST	ARGO OPERATOR TRAINING ←
			27-Jan-78	4	ST	GROUND CONTROL SURVEYING ←
			12-Jan-78	4	ST	THE SUPERVISOR & EEO
			6-Jan-78	4	ST	VESSEL TECHNOLOGY TRAINING
			21-Mar-75	4	ST	MERCHANT MARINE SAFETY SCHOOL
			1-May-74	4	GC	BUSINESS FINANCE
			1-Jan-71	2	CC	INTRODUCTION TO ADP
			1-Dec-70	2	CC	CITY SURVEYING - PART I ←
			1-Dec-70	2	CC	HYDROGRAPHIC SURVEYING ←
			1-Dec-70	2	CC	LEVELING
			1-Dec-70	2	CC	CITY SURVEYING - PART II ←
			1-Nov-70	2	CC	LINEAR SURVEYING ←

EXHIBIT 6-19

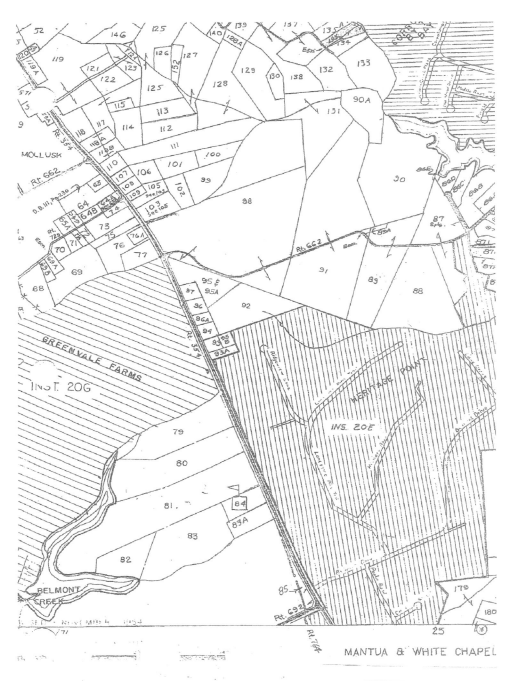

EXHIBIT 8-1

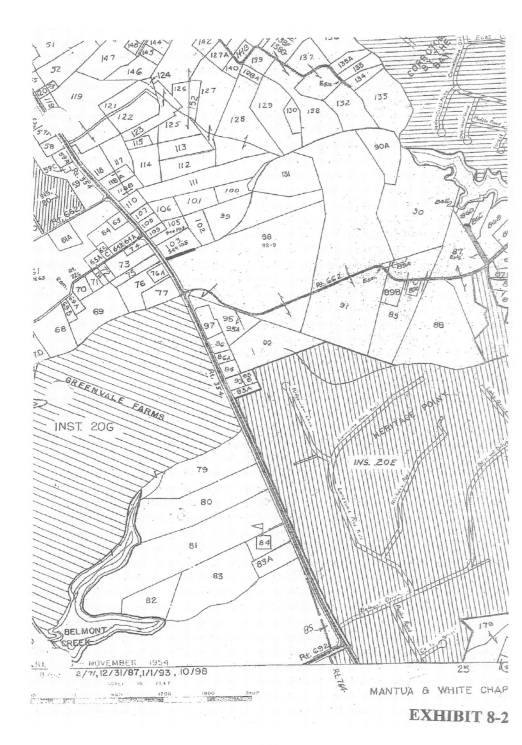

EXHIBIT 8-2

HOW COULD THIS MISREPRESENTATION HAVE BEEN UNOTICED FOR FOUR DECADES, THROUGH THREE REVISIONS, AND THREE SUBPARCEL ADDITIONS?

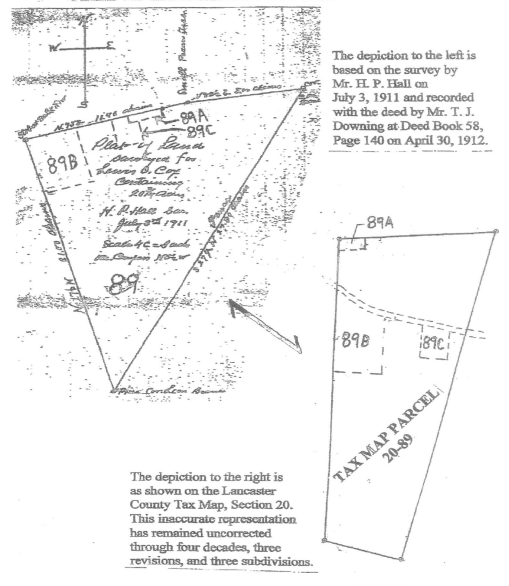

The depiction to the left is based on the survey by Mr. H. P. Hall on July 3, 1911 and recorded with the deed by Mr. T. J. Downing at Deed Book 58, Page 140 on April 30, 1912.

The depiction to the right is as shown on the Lancaster County Tax Map, Section 20. This inaccurate representation has remained uncorrected through four decades, three revisions, and three subdivisions.

EXHIBIT 8-3

A MORE CORRECT PRESENTATION OF A
PORTION OF SECTION 20, LANCASTER COUNTY
TAX MAP

Below is my drawing of a portion of Lancaster County tax map,
Section 20. The relative shapes and positions for parcels 20-87,
20-89, 20-89A, 20-89B, 20-89C, 20-90, 20-91, 20-98, 20-131, 20-
131A, and 20-131B are based on documentation on record in the
Lancaster County Records Room prior to September 11, 2014.
Parcel 20-90A is eliminated in favor of its more proper designation
as Parcel 20-131B.

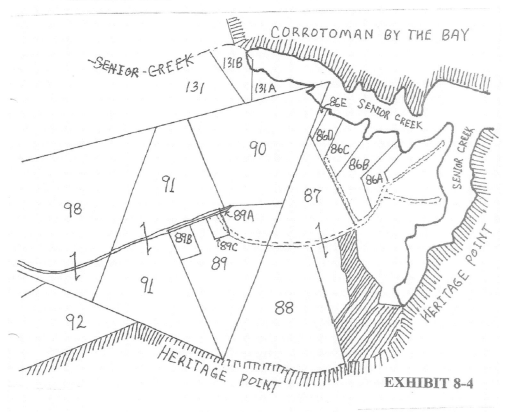

EXHIBIT 8-4

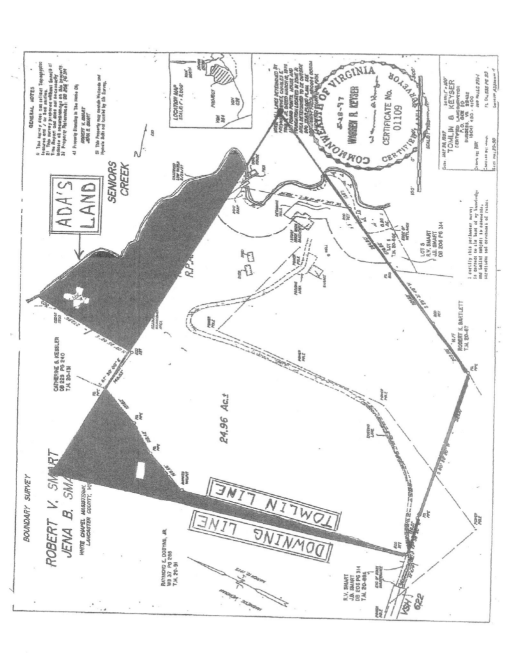

EXHIBIT 9-1

COUNTY OF LANCASTER, VIRGINIA

DIANE H. MUMFORD
CLERK OF THE CIRCUIT COURT
P.O. BOX 99
LANCASTER, VIRGINIA 22503
Phone (804) 462-5611 Fax (804) 462-9978

September 15, 2014

Mr. Robert V. Smart
561 Sage Hill Road
Lancaster, Va. 22503

RE: Courtroom sound system

Dear Mr. Smart:

Pursuant to your request for a letter regarding the sound system in the Circuit Courtroom, Mr. Steve Sorenson and myself are joining together in this one letter.

On Thursday, September 11, 2014, the case of Dobyns Family LLC vs. Robert V. Smart and Jena B. Smart was scheduled to be heard with a jury. Court opened at 9:22, the jury was sworn and jury selection commenced. The jury was seated at 9:51 and the panel for the case at hand was sworn. Opening statements were given and then Judge Michael Levy gave the jurors a comfort break at 10:16 and during that break you asked myself and Mr. Sorensen if we could turn up the sound system in the Courtroom. I informed you that the system was broken and we did not currently have a functioning sound system. Several times during the day I noticed that you were having difficulty hearing and that your hearing aid was ringing. Many of the spectators in the gallery also had difficulty hearing the proceedings. Judge Levy did ask the witnesses to speak up, but when they face a jury with no sound system the sound travels in a direction that makes it difficult to hear from the far side of the Courtroom. This has been an ongoing problem that the County is in the process of addressing, but has not yet been resolved.

I am sending a copy of this letter to the County Administrator and to the Chairman of the Board of Supervisors. This is their building and they should be aware of any problems or complaints regarding their facility.

Sincerely,

Diane H. Mumford, Clerk
Lancaster County Circuit Court

Steve Sorensen, Bailiff
Lancaster County Circuit Court

CC: County Administrator
       Chairman Board of Supervisors
       Court File

EXHIBIT 9-2

ABOUT THE AUTHOR

The author is a graduate of the United States Naval Academy, Class of 1966. He served two tours in Vietnam with the Navy before transferring his commission to the National Oceanic and Atmospheric Administration (NOAA). Early in his NOAA career the author was assigned to conduct hydrographic surveys. In preparation for this work the author was trained to accomplish geodetic survey work in order to tie hydrographic soundings to shore. This background in surveying proved useful to the author in 2013 when he began to unravel a fraud involving land boundary surveys done for him four decades earlier. The young sea-going officer pictured is the author. The picture was taken shortly after the author transferred his commission to NOAA, and near the time he purchased land in Lancaster County, Virginia.